DEVELOP YOUR
LEADERSHIP
SUPERPOWERS

"This remarkable book is packed with actionable wisdom for new and experienced leaders alike. Do not be daunted by its inclusion of 50 (!) leadership skills—each clearly described, with practical tips and room for notes—because Develop Your Leadership Superpowers offers not so much a list as an integrated set of mindsets and behaviors that can transform your work and your life."

Amy C. Edmondson, Novartis Professor of Leadership, Harvard Business School; Author, *Right Kind of Wrong: The Science of Failing Well* (Atria 2023)

"I absolutely adore Dietmar Sternad's writing style—you will feel like he is speaking directly to you (to both your heart and your mind), and this makes the book so easy and quick to read! This is my new go-to leadership book that I will be carrying copies around with me to give to my precious clients. I know they (and you) will love it, and more importantly use it, as much as I will!"

Sue Belton, Award-winning leadership coach, speaker and author (London)

"With a fresh style and inspiring illustrations and examples, Develop Your Leadership Superpowers will help you grow in 50 essential leadership skills and make a difference by achieving results and developing people. Unleash your superpowers with this book!"

Professor Daniel Pittino, Bestselling author of *The Concise Leadership Textbook: Essential Knowledge and Skills for Developing Yourself as a Leader*

"Develop Your Leadership Superpowers provides practical strategies and advice to strengthen crucial leadership abilities; covering everything from cultivating empathy and honing negotiation skills to building cohesive teams, this book offers a comprehensive yet concise leadership development program to help managers transform into impactful leaders."

Larry Cermak, CEO The Block (New York)

DEVELOP YOUR
LEADERSHIP
SUPERPOWERS

50 Key Skills You Need to
Succeed as a Leader

DIETMAR STERNAD • *Illustrated by* EVA KOBIN

econcise
Concise books for smart learners

Our mission at econcise publishing
is to create concise, approachable and affordable books
that help people become better managers and leaders.

Paperback ISBN: 978-3-903386-19-8
Hardcover ISBN: 978-3-903386-20-4
ePub ISBN: 978-3-903386-21-1
Kindle ISBN: 978-3-903386-22-8

Copy editor: Harriet Power

First published 2023 by **econcise publishing**
© 2023 econcise GmbH
Am Sonnengrund 14
A-9062 Moosburg (Austria)

www.econcise.com

Contents

Introduction

Are you just about to start **your own leadership journey**? Do you want to take your existing leadership skills to the next level? Or are you coaching others to help them become better leaders? Regardless of where you're starting from, if you are interested in **how to become more effective as a leader**, this book is for you.

When I was entrusted with my first leadership role—as a young managing director of a publishing house in my late 20s—I had no idea what to expect. There were many moments when I felt lost or insecure, such as when I had to handle conflicts, conduct tough conversations with team members, or manage other difficult situations that come along with a leadership responsibility.

Now—with 25 years of experience in various leadership roles in the fields of business and education; after endless hours of studying, teaching and writing about leadership; and having supported many other young and experienced leaders in their own leadership development in executive education, coaching and consulting—I can finally present you with the book that I wish I had read when I was at the start of my own leadership career.

In all those years, I have learned that there are no 'born' leaders. There's nothing mysterious about leadership: it is neither a magic gift from above nor rocket science. You also do not need to have a particularly outgoing or 'charismatic' personality. All you need to become a good leader is to do a few things right. And this is exactly what this book is about: it will help you to learn the **skills that really make a difference** when you are in a leadership role. When you are able to master these skills, they will become your own personal leadership superpowers.

The **50 key skills you need to succeed in a leadership role** are neatly arranged in five chapters:

- Chapter 1 is about getting into the **right leadership mindset**. Leadership always starts deep inside of you. How to develop leadership presence, become a confident and resilient leader, and control your emotions—these are just a few examples of the skills that you will learn from this chapter.
- The focus of Chapter 2 lies on **how to effectively communicate with others**. Communication is arguably the most important tool for engaging other people. We will not only explore how you can reach your communication objectives and get your message across in an effective way, but also how to listen actively, decode nonverbal signals, master negotiations and other tough conversations, and use the transformative power of feedback.
- Chapter 3 will help you **set the right priorities**, both for yourself and for your team. You will learn, for example, how to define a clear purpose, set goals, think strategically, make better decisions, solve problems in a structured way, and use clever time management strategies to focus your efforts on the things that really matter.
- The skills in Chapter 4 will enable you to **build a winning team**. We'll take a look at how you can select the right people for your team, establish trust and rapport between team members, and create and maintain a positive team spirit. You will also get tips on how to ensure accountability, hold effective team meetings, lead virtual teams, create agile teams, and deal with conflict situations.
- The best leaders **help other people grow**. Chapter 5 covers the tools for making it happen, including being able to recognize other people's strengths, providing your team members with the right challenges and development opportunities, and productively addressing performance problems. You will also learn how to use coaching as a leadership tool, effectively manage change processes, and ensure continual learning in your team.

For each of the 50 leadership skills, you will first get a quick overview of what the skill is all about and why it's important for you as a leader to become proficient in this skill. This is followed by **practical advice on how can build and enhance the skill.**

You will also get a chance to develop your leadership superpowers straight away with the **50 skill-building exercises** that you will find in this book—one for each leadership skill. Use these exercises for deliberate practice, and you will soon see progress in developing your leadership skills to a higher level.

You can use this book as a whole **master class for enhancing your leadership skills** if you decide to work through it from cover to cover. Alternatively, you can also use it as a reference book. When you are facing a new or tricky leadership situation, just turn to the relevant skill and get some inspiration for how to resolve it.

In addition to including concrete advice and practical exercises for taking your leadership skills to the next level (instead of the usual leadership blah blah), there's another thing that makes this book stand out from the crowd: Eva Kobin's heartwarming drawings that illustrate each leadership skill.

A few years ago, when Eva was my student in a master's program at our university, she started to incorporate drawings into her assignments in a leadership course. When I first saw them, I was amazed by how she was able to not only capture the essence of the course concepts, but also add a completely new emotional dimension. Looking at the drawings, you could suddenly feel what good leadership was all about rather than just understand it cognitively.

Good leaders win both minds and hearts. They are able to listen with their heart and speak to the heart—just like the little 'superhero leader' in Eva's pictures.

And please don't forget to always look for the little cookie-chasing dog in the drawings too. If it makes you smile, take it as a reminder not to take everything too seriously—especially in your leadership role. Wise leaders know that humor is a great tool for building deeper relationships.

A dog is also a faithful companion, and Eva and I very much hope that this book will become a faithful companion on your personal leadership journey too. So let's get started with developing your leadership superpowers! (And don't forget to share cookies with your team along the way.)

Develop a leadership mindset

This chapter will enable you to:

» Adopt the attitude of a leader.
» Connect authentically with other people, giving them the feeling that you really care about them.
» Control your emotions and show confidence (particularly in difficult situations).
» Spread positive energy in your team.
» Harness the power of self-reflection.

Leadership always begins **inside yourself**—with how you think and feel. When you feel confident inside, you will be able to instill confidence in others. When you approach other people with positive energy, you will be imbued with energy in return. And when you really care about a common goal, your team members will start caring too. Your attitude as a leader will have a tremendous effect on the attitude of the people around you.

As every successful athlete knows, to win the championship, you first need to **win your inner game**. Let us therefore explore in this first chapter how you can develop the right **leadership mindset**—the attitudes and beliefs that shape your habits as a leader and will therefore determine whether you succeed in your leadership role.

Among other skills, you will learn how to make others feel important (this is one of the secrets of effective leadership), control your emotions (instead of being controlled by them), and come back stronger when you are faced with problems and disappointments. Taken together, the skills in this chapter will help you develop a positive leadership mindset that will encourage others to believe in you and give their best.

01 Develop leadership presence

What does developing leadership presence mean?

Some people seem to naturally command the attention of others. They have got what is called **leadership presence**: "the ability to connect authentically with the thoughts and feelings of others."[1]

Leadership presence is not about presenting yourself in the best possible light (although speaking and acting with passion can play a certain role here). At its core, it is about **making another person feel that they are the most important person in the room** through showing them that you are fully focused on them.

Why is leadership presence an important leadership skill?

Leadership presence can help you to **mobilize and influence others**. People will pay attention to you, and it will make it easier for you to reach the results that you would like to achieve together with others.

You've likely heard that **charisma** is often considered to be an important quality of exceptional leaders. You've got charisma when others feel almost 'magnetically' attracted to you.

People are not born with charisma, however (although most babies are actually quite good in drawing the attention of everyone around toward them). There's no magic involved here either. As Olivia Fox Cabane, who has extensively studied the phenomenon of charisma, explains, it is simply "a result of specific nonverbal behaviors."[2] The most important of those behaviors (or, in the words of Fox Cabane, the "real core component of charisma"[3]) is **showing others that you are fully present.**

How do you develop leadership presence?

Presence is not a trait, it's a behavior. In essence, it means **being fully aware of what's going on around you**, and strongly connecting with the world and people around you. In a leadership context, it particularly means **paying undivided attention** to the people you are with.

It sounds simple, but for most of us, that's quite a challenge because we get distracted so easily, especially by our own thoughts. When your mind is drifting away (e.g. if you're thinking about what you're going to say next before the person you're talking to has finished speaking), you are unable to make deep connections with others. People will notice when you are not fully with them, for example because they unconsciously detect that your facial reactions are just few milliseconds delayed.

Here are a few tips about **how to create full presence**, the key ingredient of charisma:[4]

- When you are interacting with others, **regularly check whether you are in the moment**: whether you are paying full attention to them. If you notice that your mind is drifting away, try to bring yourself back to the present moment.
- Make **good eye contact**—show the other person that you are really interested in connecting with them.
- Use **mirroring**, matching your body language to the other person. It's a powerful way of connecting more deeply with others.
- Carefully **take note of what others say, do, or express with their body and face** (see also *Skill 15 Decode nonverbal signals*). It will

give you clues about what they think and how they feel. These clues will help you to adequately react to other people's needs, which in turn gives them the feeling that you care about them.

- **Don't email or surf on the web** when you're on the phone with someone. Keep in mind that they will notice that split-second delay in your reactions (and they most likely won't appreciate hearing you type).

Leadership presence is not so much about how you are presenting yourself—it is about your ability to recognize and appreciate the thoughts and feelings of others. That said, it certainly helps to show some confidence in a leadership role—so let us explore this next.

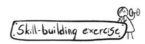

Developing leadership presence

Next time you are holding a conversation with a colleague, friend or family member, try to fully concentrate on the other person. Use mirroring and eye contact. Be aware when you are getting distracted, and refocus your full attention on what the other person has to say (both verbally and non-verbally). Try to understand what's important to them and how they are feeling.

Keep only one big goal in mind for the conversation: to let the other person feel that they have your exclusive and undivided attention.

My personal notes about developing leadership presence

_____

_____

_____

_____

02 Show confidence

What does showing confidence mean?

Confidence is the feeling of trust in someone (in the case of self-confidence, it's the feeling of trust in yourself). It comes in two different forms: (a) **confidence in your abilities**—the belief that you will be able to do something well, and (b) **interpersonal confidence**, which is being comfortable interacting with others without anxiety. Both aspects of confidence are important components of what is called **mental toughness**: the ability to handle difficult situations well.[5]

Why is showing confidence an important leadership skill?

Confidence signals competence. When you appear confident—when you give other people the feeling that you have little doubt in your ability to deal with a situation—it will be easier for them to develop trust in you. Most people don't like uncertainty. Showing confidence as a leader will help to reduce doubts and uncertainty, and it will also contribute to increasing the overall level of confidence in your team.

If you are being seen as hesitant, in contrast, if you show anxiety, and if you do not believe in yourself—why should others believe in you?

A higher level of confidence will also affect **your ability to deal with setbacks.**[6] This is especially important when things are getting a bit tougher for your team. When your team members feel that you as a leader are still calm and forward-looking in the face of difficulties, it can help them to remain or become more confident too.

Be careful, however, not to appear over-confident. There is a thin line between very high confidence and hubris. Beware of the **'Icarus effect'** of believing in abilities you do not have.[7]

How do you show confidence?

There are three ways in which you can show confidence. One is **with words**. That's arguably the weakest one. People may believe you if you tell them that you are confident about something, but they may not, especially if you do not *sound* confident.

The second way of showing confidence is a stronger one. It is about *how* **you speak**. More confident people usually speak less, more slowly, and with deliberate pauses (especially before they say something). At the end of their sentences, they lower the intonation of their voice, thus conveying "vocal power."[8]

The third way of showing confidence is through your **body language**. That's the strongest signal for others, because people can actually see (consciously or unconsciously) how confident you are. Just watch a troop of monkeys, and you will quickly recognize, just from watching their body language, who's the alpha leader.

You can easily project confidence with an upright and open posture, a relaxed face, eye contact, and a firm handshake. Hiding your hands in your pockets, crossing your arms or legs, excessive nodding (*"Look how eager I am!"*) and fidgeting with your clothes, hair or nose will have the opposite effect.

Several leadership coaches recommend the use of 'power posing,' where you spend one or two minutes making 'powerful' or 'expansive' postures (e.g. putting your fist in the air and loudly saying 'Yes' to yourself before entering a meeting room) for helping you to feel more confident.

Although researchers still disagree on the effects power poses have on your emotions and bodily state, there are quite some people who find them a useful tool to put themselves in a more confident state of mind (in the sense of "fake it 'til you make it").[9]

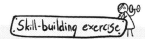

Conveying confidence through your voice

Use the following tips for conveying confidence through your voice in your next conversation (or presentation):[10]

1. **Speak slowly and clearly.** Give others the feeling that every single word you're saying counts.
2. **Use pauses.** A pause will give you time to take a deep and calming breath, underlines that what you are saying is important, and shows that you are confident that you will not be interrupted.
3. **Lower your intonation at the end of a sentence.** Try to read a sentence once with your voice going up, then a second time with your voice going down. You will instantly notice the difference.

My personal notes about showing confidence

03 Spread positive energy

What does spreading positive energy mean?

Spreading positive energy (and generally being a 'positive leader') means being **optimistic and hopeful about the future.**[11] As a positive leader, you will deliberately try to stay in a committed, passionate state of mind, which will also inspire your team members. Instead of complaining how bad things are, you will adopt a 'can-do' mindset and see challenges as an opportunity for taking charge and changing things for the better.

Why is spreading positive energy an important leadership skill?

As a leader, you are setting the tone for your team. It will make a big difference for the people around you whether you come across as negative, grumpy and annoyed, or as positive, friendly and uplifting. Researchers have found ample evidence for the contagious effect of a leader's mood and emotions on their team, and observed that the contagion of emotions between leader and followers "is directly linked to leader effectiveness and performance."[12]

Do you want your team to be committed, achievement- and solution-oriented and confident? Then keep in mind that your state as a leader influences everyone around you, too. Your personal energy level will be mirrored in the energy level of your team.

How do you spread positive energy?

Here's what you as a leader can do to be a 'superspreader' of positive energy for your team:

- **Adopt a positive state of mind before you start interacting with others.** Remind yourself that it is your job as a leader to create a positive, forward-looking atmosphere. Even if you are tired, try to show your best self in front of others. Make a conscious decision to be positive and show them how much you care. Sometimes, it takes some effort, but it will reap rewards as you will get a lot of positive energy back from your team in return.
- **Use the power of positive recognition.** Take notice when someone is doing good work, and tell them how much you appreciate it. Share success stories within the team and harness the power of praise.
- **Use positive words.** Say 'energized' instead of 'nervous,' 'learning' instead of 'failure,' 'blessed with a lot of work' instead of 'stressed,' and 'great' instead of 'okay.'[13] Words are powerful tools that help to define reality.
- **Think in solutions rather than problems.** Ask questions like *"Which options do we have to solve this in the best possible way?"* or *"What can we do to address this challenge?"* to focus the team on making progress. Maybe you could even make a 'no complaining or blaming' agreement with your team to prevent them from sliding into a spiral of negativity.
- **Smile.** That's one of the most powerful tools for a leader to spread positive energy. As Louis Armstrong and Dean Martin sang, "when you're smiling, the whole world smiles with you."

Having a positive attitude is a deliberate choice—a choice that can have an immensely positive effect on the motivation, relationships, and ability of your team to solve problems and achieve your joint goals.

Spreading positive energy

Next time you feel that you are not in a peak state, maybe because someone or something just annoyed you, try out the following steps to help you get into a positive mental state again:

1. **Take a deep breath.** Fully focus on your breathing, noticing how the air is flowing in and out. Feel how it connects you with the world: the place where you can make a positive impact with a positive attitude right now.
2. **Focus your mind on good things.** When you feel discomfort, think about things that you value or love—a smile from a loved one, an ability that you are proud of, or something that you really appreciate or are grateful for about your work or life. That will get you into a more positive state of mind.
3. **Use positive self-talk.** *"Yes, I can do this," "This is a great opportunity for me to learn...," "I will give my very best,"* or *"I will show them how much I care as a leader"*—positive affirmations like these can help you to get into the right state of mind.
4. **Smile**—even if you don't feel like it. With your smile, you not only signal to others that you are friendly and positive—research has shown that smiling can actually reduce your own stress levels too.[14]

My personal notes about spreading positive energy

04 Show that you care

What does it mean to show that you care?

As a caring leader, you will **give your team members the feeling that they are really important to you**—as individuals, not only as a 'human resource'—and that you want them to succeed and thrive. Heather Younger, author of *The Art of Caring Leadership*, defines caring leadership as "taking daily actions in ways that show concern and kindness to those we lead."[15]

Why is showing care an important leadership skill?

There are countless stories of people who quit their jobs because their bosses just didn't care about them. Without doubt, you will never want to become such a terrible boss!

As a caring leader, you will try your best to make your team members feel supported, appreciated and valued. When people feel valued, it not only lowers the chance that they will jump ship—it will also have an impact on their engagement at work. Researchers found evidence for a link between benevolent leadership and the performance levels of followers.[16] As Melissa Houston writes in a Forbes article, "there is a direct correlation between the treatment of employees and their productivity."[17]

How do you show that you care?

As you strive to become a caring leader, you will first and foremost want to **avoid being a careless leader**, meaning, according to Heather Younger, that you will not do any of the following:[18]

- Not responding to employee requests.
- Micromanaging people with an excessive level of control and supervision.
- Not giving your team members the opportunity to grow and advance in their career.
- Playing favorites.
- Just caring about performance targets, and not about how people feel.
- Letting others feel that you are 'the boss' (e.g. not giving them a voice in a meeting or interrupting them while they're speaking).

Avoiding carelessness is a good first step, but needs to be complemented by **actively caring behavior** if you would like to be seen as a leader who really cares:[19]

- **Respond in a timely manner** when team members need something from you.
- **Take your time to ask team members how they are,** what they have enjoyed over the weekend, how their family members are. Give them the feeling that you are interested in them as whole people who also live a life outside of the office.
- **Ask your team members for advice** and involve them in decision-making processes. People who are given a voice tend to be a lot more committed to the decisions that are being made. Let them feel that their opinion matters.
- **Give people your full attention and listen attentively** (see also Skills *01 Develop leadership presence* and *14 Practice active listening*). You

can even take notes when they speak in order to show them how much you care about what they have to say.

- **Empower your team members.** Within the boundaries of a well-defined purpose and clear expectations, give them your full trust and the autonomy to make their own decisions and do things in their own way. Make sure they have the opportunity to think and act independently instead of being patronized.

As an attentive and caring leader, you will also notice when someone is not feeling well and is therefore not able to work at the highest performance level. We all have our ups and downs, and we need people who have a sympathetic ear and support us in phases when things are getting a bit more difficult.

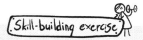

Showing how much you care

The next time you have a one-on-one meeting with a team member, try to show them during the meeting that you care about them. Ask them how they are, and show interest in both their work priorities and their private life. Try to really understand and value their beliefs, thoughts, passions, or fears. Make them feel, through giving them your full attention, that they are the most important person for you in this moment.

My personal notes about showing how much I care

05 Cultivate a growth mindset

What does it mean to cultivate a growth mindset?

A growth mindset is the belief that **you can always develop your abilities to a higher level** with the right amount of dedication and deliberate practice. The opposite is a fixed mindset, when you believe that people have innate talents, abilities and intelligence that cannot be changed or improved.[20]

There are two ways of cultivating a growth mindset as a leader: first, for yourself, through committing yourself to continually improving your leadership skills day by day. And second, for your team members, through believing in their ability to learn and develop new skills, and providing them with opportunities to grow.

Why is cultivating a growth mindset an important leadership skill?

Research findings indicate that "improving leadership competencies is more likely to occur when managers hold a growth mindset."[21] That's actually quite logical: if you believe that it's possible to grow as a leader, you will put more effort into improving your leadership skills—for example, into consciously trying out new approaches (like the ones you can find in this book), reflecting, or learning. That will almost inevitably help you to become a better leader. How you think about yourself will have a strong impact on your actions—as well as on your performance. Believe that you can grow, and you will start doing the right things that will actually allow you to grow.

It's exactly the same with your team members. If you believe in their ability to develop, you will start to provide them with the right development opportunities (see also *Skill 43 Provide challenges*). And it will just feel great to see your whole team grow too.

How do you cultivate a growth mindset?

Here are three key steps for getting yourself into a growth mindset:

- **Believe in your ability to learn.** Whatever your current skill level, there's always a higher level that you can reach when you are just willing to put in enough effort. Make it a habit to add the word 'yet' to the end of sentences, so that, for example, *'I am not good at giving presentations'* becomes *'I am not good at giving presentations yet.'*
- **Embrace challenges.** In every difficult situation, even in those that some people call a 'failure,' lies an opportunity for self-improvement. So don't try to avoid challenges: leave your comfort zone and actively look for them instead! Challenges will push you to develop your skills to the next level.
- **Enjoy the learning process.** Of course, as a manager or leader, you should be focused on results. But at the same time, don't forget to enjoy the view along the way, even when there are setbacks or obstacles on the road to success. Set your mind on what you could improve and how you will improve it, try it out, learn on the way, and celebrate the progress that you are making on your learning journey.

What works for developing your personal growth mindset can also be translated into your role as a team leader: believe in your team members' ability to learn, provide them with challenges that will allow them to grow, and recognize and appreciate their learning progress as much as the results that they achieve. Believe in their growth—and watch them grow!

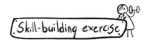

Cultivating a growth mindset

When you write your daily to-do list, set yourself **one learning goal for the day.** For example, if you're planning to hold a one-to-one meeting with a team member, you can set yourself the goal of practicing your active listening skills. Maybe you want to try out some strategies for improving your presentation skills in the next team meeting, or use a new tool in a decision-making process (you will find a lot of other ideas for what you could learn or improve as a leader in this book too).

Making your daily learning goal explicit will prime your mind for learning. It will remind you that you can deliberately learn something new every day, and that there's always room for improvement and growth.

In addition to setting your daily learning goals, keep a **learning diary.** Take a few minutes to write down your 'number one learning of the day.' It can be linked to your daily learning goal, but it might also be something else that you have learned on that day. Writing down your key learnings every day is a way to praise yourself for the progress you are making on your journey to developing your personal leadership superpowers. It will also be a powerful reminder of your ability to improve yourself every single day.

My personal notes about cultivating a growth mindset

06 Control your emotions

What does it mean to control your emotions?

Emotional control is the ability to **recognize and manage your emotions,** keep your fears and anxieties in check, and deliberately decide on the extent to which you would (or wouldn't) like to reveal your emotional state to others.[22] Being able to control your emotions does not mean suppressing them altogether, but consciously deciding how to respond to the emotions which inevitably arise within you.

Why is controlling your emotions an important leadership skill?

There are plenty of opportunities to get emotional in a leadership role. It's easy to get anxious, frustrated or angry when things do not work out as planned, when other people fail to hold their promises, or when members of your team are getting emotional in conflict situations (as negative emotions can become highly contagious).

Let's face it—we are all emotional beings. As humans, we are hardwired in such a way that we always experience emotions *before* we are able to think rationally about something that we experience. It's an automatic reaction; that's just how our brain works. What we can influence, however, is how we deal with the emotions that we're experiencing, and this can make a big difference to how we are seen by others.

Ideally, as a leader, you will want to be seen as someone who is able to **stay calm and maintain a positive outlook in stressful situations**. That will give your team members a sense of safety. Keeping a cool head when making difficult decisions, finding adequate solutions in emotionally charged conflict situations, avoiding intimidating others with emotional outbursts, and not infecting your team members with your own worries and fears (yes, we all have them!)—these are all very important qualities that people look for in their leaders.

As with all other leaders in this world, you will have emotions too. As an effective leader, however, you will learn not to be controlled by your emotions, but to bring your emotions under your own control instead.

How do you control your emotions?

Professor Steve Peters, a consultant psychiatrist to many peak performers, from Olympic champions to the football stars of Liverpool FC, makes the following suggestions for **managing our inner 'chimp'** (that's what he calls the emotional system in our brain):[23]

1. **Recognize when your thinking is being hijacked by your emotional system** (ask yourself 'Do I want these feelings?'—when the answer is 'no,' then it's an emotion that you want to address). You could, for example, train yourself to say a word like 'STOP' or 'CHANGE' when you experience a strong negative feeling, to signal to your mind that you intend to change your response to the emotion.

2. **Express your emotion.** 'Getting it off your chest' helps your inner 'chimp' to calm down. Ideally, you won't do that in front of your team members, but in private (that's why it might make sense to escape from the situation first), or with the right person who you trust at your side. Before you let your emotions out, it's almost impossible to think rationally about a certain issue (that's also important to remember, by the way, when you communicate with other people who are getting emotional).

3. **Put things into perspective.** Ask yourself questions like 'How important will this be in a few years from now?' or 'Do I really need to worry about things I cannot control?' Even if you might not be able to change the situation, you can at least change your attitude toward it.

4. **Ask 'how' instead of 'why'.** Instead of ruminating on why all those bad things always happen to you, make a plan of how you will deal with your feelings and how you will move forward. Find someone who you trust to talk through your plans. Talking can help you to cope with stress and negative emotions.

5. **Smile.** As long as a situation is not really having a huge impact on your whole life, smiling can be your 'secret weapon' for getting yourself into a more positive mental state again (see also *Skill 03 Spread positive energy*).

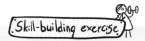

Your plan for controlling your emotions

Create a plan for dealing with negative emotions when they suddenly arise. Write down what you will do, and then rehearse it in your mind.[24] How will you remind yourself to slow down a bit (e.g. by saying 'STOP' to yourself, or by taking a deep breath)? How will you express your emotions? What will you ask yourself to put things into perspective?

Practice what you will do in your mind several times, so that you will be well prepared to act according to your plan in the next emotionally charged situation.

My personal notes about controlling my emotions

07 Know your values

What does knowing your values mean?

Values are lasting beliefs that you (or others) hold about **what is important in life and at work**, and about what is desirable or undesirable. Our values have a strong influence on our choices and behavior. We use them—both consciously and unconsciously—for making decisions, justifying our actions, and judging how we or others should behave.[25]

Values are usually developed in a process of socialization, through learning what others around us (from our first caregivers to our current co-workers) deem acceptable or not. As we have all been socialized in different environments, both our individual and group values can significantly differ.

Making your values explicit can help you a lot in your leadership role, not only for making better decisions (which is much easier when you know what's important to you and what isn't), but also in providing orientation for your team. Your team members will understand you and your actions much better when they know what you stand for.

Why is knowing your values an important leadership skill?

Knowing your values will enable you to **lead with more clarity**. Values can act as a compass that will show you and your team members the right direction, especially in difficult situations. If you make your values explicit, it will be easier to understand why you decide or act in a particular way, and why this is important for you and for the organization.

When you live according to your own values, you will come across as an **authentic leader**. With strong ethical values, you will also convey a deep sense of **integrity**. Both authenticity and integrity are important characteristics of well-regarded leaders.

Knowing your personal values will also enable you to compare them with the core values of your organization. Make sure that your personal values and the organizational values are aligned with each other. After all, why should your team members believe in and behave according to the organizational values if you don't do so as a leader?

How do you know your values?

The following three steps can help you better understand your values:

1. **Identify your values.** There are several ways of identifying what is really important to you. Think about what makes you really happy, when you've been really proud of yourself, or what gives you meaning in your life. Why do you admire the people who you admire the most? Or take a look at a comprehensive list of values and select the ones that are most important to you (see the exercise on the next page).
2. **Prioritize your values.** If you have identified a couple of values that are really important to you, weigh them against each other. Which one matters more to you? Rank your values so that you know which one has precedence when they come into conflict with each other.
3. **Test your values.** Ask yourself if you would be comfortable with telling your values to the people you admire the most. And would you still support these values when your choice will make you unpopular and puts you in the minority?[26]

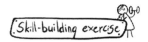

Knowing your values

Take a look at the list of values below. Draw a circle around the five values which you consider to be the most important ones for you personally. You can also add additional values in the lines below the list.

Achievement	Cooperation	Improvement	Recognition
Advancement	Courage	Independence	Responsibility
Authenticity	Empathy	Individuality	Service orientation
Autonomy	Equality	Influence	Status
Balance	Excellence	Innovation	Success
Care for others	Fairness	Integrity	Sustainability
Community	Flexibility	Optimism	Transparency
Compassion	Harmony	Power	Wealth
Competence	Honesty	Professionalism	Winning
Credibility	Humility	Quality orientation	Wisdom

_____   _____   _____   _____

_____   _____   _____   _____

Take the five values that you selected from the list above. Try to rank them from 1 to 5 according to how important these values are to you, starting with the most important one as number 1.[27]

My personal notes about knowing my values

_____

_____

_____

08 Be fully committed

What does it mean to be fully committed?

Being committed means **making a promise**, both to others and to your-self, to fully engage yourself for a certain purpose, and **being determined to keep this promise.**[28]

A commitment always consists of two parts: first, **goal orientation**—the decision to do what it takes to achieve a certain goal that is important for your team or organization; and second, the **pledge not to give up** when you are facing obstacles, and to try your hardest to find solutions for all the challenges and obstacles that occur on the way.

Real commitment shows in your actions as a leader, not merely in your words. Are you willing to make a sacrifice when you are facing obstacles or resistance? Will you continue to pursue your goal, even when you are confronted with setbacks? Will you keep your promise?

Why is being committed an important leadership skill?

Commitment means that you are willing to dedicate a lot of time and energy to ensuring the success of an important cause. It's actually not possible to be a leader without being committed to something. Why should anyone want to follow you if you are not showing any dedication to a worthwhile cause.

It is through **commitment**—and its even more intense twin, **passion**—that you as a leader inspire other people. When you are fully committed to something, you will create positive, goal-oriented energy. Your mental state will influence the people around you. When the team feels the leader's energy, they will respond, and you will be able to create momentum toward the goal.

Researchers have found evidence for an **emotional contagion effect** between a leader's work passion and their team members' inclination to also invest time and energy in working toward a certain goal. The strength of this 'commitment transfer effect' is influenced, however, by what is called 'goal content congruence': the degree to which the leader's goal is also important for the team members.[29]

In addition to having a positive influence on your team members, a high level of commitment toward a certain goal or cause will also help you to persist in the face of difficulties and stick to your goals, thus improving your chances of eventually achieving them.

How do you become fully committed?

You can take the following five steps to fully commit yourself to a certain goal:

1. **Set a goal that is worth following.** You need to know what you would like to achieve, and also why that's important for you, for your team, and for your organization. Reminding yourself (and others) of the 'why' will help you to stay committed.
2. **Understand what you need to do to get it done.** Remember that being committed is ultimately about your actions. Make sure that you know exactly what you need to *do*: which action you will take in order to achieve what you want to achieve. Try to identify the potential hurdles and obstacles, and make a plan to overcome them.

3. **Make yourself accountable.** Tell other people which action you will take to make it happen, or at least write down what you will do and when, so that you are accountable to yourself. Regularly check your progress (or agree with others to have your progress checked at a certain deadline).
4. **Celebrate small victories.** Reward yourself and your team members, for example with praise or a little celebration, not only for achieving a goal, for also for *doing the right things* that need to be done in order to bring you closer to your goals.

Staying fully committed

The first part of *getting committed*—of setting a goal and promising to yourself that you will take all the action that is necessary to achieve it— is the easier part of the commitment journey. The second part is usually much more difficult: *staying committed*, even when you are facing distractions, obstacles, opposition or other difficulties.

The next time you're setting yourself an important goal, try to use the following two **commitment boosters:**[30]

1. Use a **commitment tracker.** In its simplest form, it's just a calendar in which you tick off every day when you have kept your commitment. You know that at the end of the day, you will be accountable to yourself. The number of Xs in the boxes will show you at one glance how successful you have been in keeping your commitment.
2. Get an **accountability partner.** Tell a friend, colleague or other trusted person what you will do and when you will report back to them about whether you have kept your commitment.

My personal notes about being and staying fully committed

_____

_____

09 Be resilient

What does it mean to be resilient?

Resilience is the ability to **return to a positive state of mind** after something difficult has happened to you. As a resilient leader, you are able to adapt to challenging circumstances and **bounce back** from failures and disappointments.

It is absolutely normal to initially become anxious, worried, or frustrated when things do not turn out as planned. It is your choice, however, how you then deal with these difficult situations: whether you let yourself be dragged down and feel pity for yourself, or hold your head high and return to showing your best self again.

Why is being resilient an important leadership skill?

Every leader faces setbacks. Life is full of friction. You cannot expect that everything will always work out as you would like it to. As a leader, you will be faced with conflicts, people who do not like what you do, or unexpected events that will make it more challenging or even impossible for you to reach your goals. There are good and bad times, and it's especially during the bad times when you can show your real leadership qualities.

How you act during a crisis situation will send a clear signal to your team members (they are always watching you, no matter if you want them to or not). If you show your frustration, chances are high that they will become frustrated too. It is your responsibility as a leader to create a positive outlook, to be a role model, to show that it is possible to cope with stressful and difficult situations, and to move forward again.

How do you become resilient?

Here's what you can do to become a more resilient leader:

- **Expect friction.** Don't assume that everything will always turn out as planned. In a dynamic and uncertain world, it is impossible to keep everything under control. Expect that difficult situations will arise, and you will be better prepared to deal with them (ideally, have a plan ready for those difficulties that are most likely to occur).
- **Accept what you cannot change.** Some things we can control. There's no need to worry about these things, because we have the power to make them better: we can take action to move in a positive direction. Other things are not in our control. Again, there's no need to worry here either, as we can't change the situation (and worrying harder won't make any difference). In this case, it's best to simply accept what's happened.
- **Tell yourself that there are no bad situations, only new ones**—and in these new situations, it's your responsibility as a leader to always give your best. There's no excuse for spreading negativity. Making the best out of every situation—that's what you are here for as a leader.
- **Recognize the opportunity that lies in adversity.** Every mistake or failure is a chance to learn; every setback is an opportunity to show your commitment and integrity. In the end, success does not lie in achieving every goal, but in living up to your values.

"A loss isn't a loss if you learn something as a result of it,"[31] says leadership expert John Maxwell in his book *Sometimes You Win, Sometimes You*

Learn. Do you want to be a loser or a learner? It's your choice—a choice that you can make every time anew when you are facing obstacles and difficulties in your leadership role.

Your personal resilience plan

It will always be easier to face adversity with a prepared mind. The following steps will help you develop your personal resilience plan, which you can then apply in the next crisis situation:

1. **Learn from how you mastered prior challenges.** Recall where you have already experienced a significant setback in your life. What helped you to overcome the challenge? Use three different categories here: *people* who supported you, *thoughts* that you found helpful to get back into a more positive mood, and *actions* that you took to deal with the situation (maybe it helped you to distance yourself from the situation, to reflect about it in a journal, or just to take a long walk). Also think about what you learned from the challenge and which new opportunities arose from it.
2. **Use your learnings to develop a plan for dealing with the next crisis situation.** Write down which people you will turn to for support, which thinking strategies you will use (e.g. to see the situation just as a 'new' one rather as a 'bad' one), and which actions you will take to get yourself back into a positive state of mind again.

My personal notes about being resilient

10 Make self-reflection a habit

What does self-reflection mean?

Self-reflection (or 'personal reflection') is the process of **consciously look-ing at, thinking about, and learning from your own attitudes, actions, and experiences as a leader** with the aim of improving your effective-ness in the leadership role. It's one of the most important ways to learn, develop yourself, and grow as a leader.

Why is self-reflection an important leadership skill?

Researchers found that "the habit of reflection can separate extraordinary professionals from mediocre ones."[32]

Extraordinary leaders know the value of **pressing the 'pause' button** from time to time. They take regular time-outs from their busy schedule to deliberately reflect on their actions and their consequences. During these time-outs, they think about what worked well (and why), and—even more importantly—which of their actions did not lead to a desired result, and what they can improve in future.

Reflecting on things that surprise us (because we expected a different outcome), frustrate us (when we do not get what we want), or that we consider to be a failure (when we are unable to meet either our own or others' expectations) have proved to be particularly useful for learning and developing oneself in a leadership role.[33]

In addition to the immense **learning effect** (self-reflection was also called "the foundation that all other soft skills grow from"[34]), researchers found that self-reflection can have an **energizing effect** on leaders.[35]

A regular practice of personal reflection will help you form a realistic image of yourself, understand your strengths and limitations, and develop your leadership skills to a higher level.

How do you become effective in self-reflection?

There are four steps to ensure that you can fully harness the power of self-reflection:

1. **Make it a habit.** Reserve time for self-reflection on a continual basis. Find a quiet place without distractions and set aside 10 to 15 minutes every day, half an hour per week, or two hours at the end of each quarter of the year. Whatever your preferred timeframe, it's important to reflect regularly. This will enable constant and steady progress in improving your leadership skills.
2. **Write it down.** Keep a journal to record your thoughts in written form. Writing forces you to think slowly and clearly, and when you put things on paper, they are outside of your head, and therefore easier to challenge in a more objective way. Although some people prefer to use a computer, writing by hand is usually the best choice for fully engaging your mind.
3. **Look back and learn.** Begin your reflection session with a look back. What have you experienced in your leadership role since the last reflection meeting with yourself? What worked well—and why? Which actions led to a different outcome than you expected—and what could be the reasons for that? Be honest with yourself! Don't

blame it on others when something went wrong. Think about your own role instead. And don't forget to ask yourself the crucial question: *"What do I learn from this?"*

4. **Look forward.** Based on what you have learned from your reflection, how will you approach things differently in future? Be specific: *"When I will face situation X, I will ..."* Clearly define your priorities—especially your learning priorities—for the next period (day, week, quarter).

Reflecting on critical incidents

Use the following simple yet powerful three-questions model to reflect on and learn from any critical incident that you are facing as a leader:[36]

1. **'What?'** Describe what happened. What are the facts, and which feelings did you (and others) have?
2. **'So what?'** Explore the meaning of what happened. Why did it happen? What can you learn from the incident? What does it tell you about yourself, your attitude, and the way you act and work?
3. **'Now what?'** Develop an action plan for how you will do things differently (or better) next time you are faced with a similar situation.

My personal notes about making self-reflection a habit

Communicate with impact

This chapter will enable you to:

» Engage others by communicating clearly and effectively with them.
» Enhance your active listening skills and your ability to decode body language.
» Present your ideas to others in a convincing way.
» Use constructive feedback to help others make progress.
» Confidently handle difficult conversations and negotiations.

You can only influence other people as a leader if you're able to connect well with them through effective communication. Therefore, to become an effective leader, you must first and foremost become an effective communicator.

The root of the word 'communication' lies in the Latin *communicare*, which means 'to share.' And that's what good leadership communication is all about: you need to be able to share thoughts, ideas and information, and above all **create shared meaning**. Sharing (as well as communicating) is always a two-way process, which involves effort on both the sender and the receiver sides.

In this chapter you will learn the leadership communication skills that you need on both sides. It is not enough for you as a leader to become proficient in presenting your ideas to others in a persuasive way: as an effective communicator, you will also be able to listen actively and attentively—especially to nonverbal behavior and what is not explicitly said—to really understand what other people want to share with you.

Leadership is not a monologue but a **dialogue**, and this chapter prepares you to have fruitful dialogues with other people, including in more difficult conversation situations (e.g. when you need to give negative feedback, deal with conflict situations, or conduct tough negotiations).

11 Respect self-esteem needs

What does respecting self-esteem needs mean?

Self-esteem is **the belief that someone holds about their self-worth:** the respect that they have for themselves and their abilities. Everything that you say or do as a leader can have an impact on other people's self-esteem. Ideally, as a leader, you will communicate in a way that has a positive impact on the self-esteem of your team members.

Why is respecting self-esteem needs an important leadership skill?

To achieve a high level of performance, your team members need to believe in themselves and their abilities. In other words, they need a high level of self-esteem to perform well. As a leader, you can have a strong influence on the self-esteem of your team members, especially through the way you communicate with them.

The renowned psychologist and communication theorist Paul Watzlawick reminds us that **every communication has both a content aspect**

and a relational aspect (with the latter determining the former).[1] Let's assume you have just received critical feedback from a good friend who wants to support you. You would most probably interpret the feedback very differently than if it came from a colleague who is always very critical of you.

Just as the relationship determines how a message will be received, with every communication you are also sending a message about the relationship. The other person will not only hear what you say, but also evaluate (unconsciously) *how* you say something. The way in which you communicate will either lead to an increase in their level of self-esteem (e.g. when you highlight their strengths, or ask them for advice) or decrease their self-esteem (e.g. when you give direct instructions through which you convey that you are 'the boss').

If you hurt the self-esteem of others too much in a conversation (e.g. when you tell someone that their idea is 'total crap'), you will limit their ability to contribute, as the negative emotions that you are causing will override their capacity to think straightly. At the same time, you will also hurt your relationship with that person, as we all tend to develop negative feelings toward people who attack our self-esteem.

How do you ensure that you respect others' self-esteem needs?

Here's what you can do as a leader to strengthen the self-esteem of your team members:

- Be aware that in every conversation, **people will (unconsciously) evaluate whether you see them in a positive or negative way.** How you communicate will always have an impact on their self-esteem. Whenever you communicate with others, therefore, make sure you try to respect and build their self-esteem. Give them your full attention, and carefully choose your words in a way that gives them the feeling that you see them in a positive light.
- Always **try to avoid mocking remarks and direct attacks** on other people.
- Instead of giving instructions, **share observations and information** (e.g. *"I recognized that last year's numbers aren't currently included in the presentation"* instead of *"Include last year's numbers in the presen-*

tation!").[2] This helps to avoid your team members feeling like they are being bossed around. Treat them as equals, not as inferiors!

- Words of **appreciation and recognition** can work wonders to build the self-esteem of other people, as can honest requests for advice.

Every conversation is an opportunity not only for getting a message across, but also for strengthening the self-esteem of another person, and at the same time also strengthening your relationship with them.

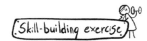

Respecting self-esteem needs

Hold a conversation with a colleague, friend or family member with the clear goal of strengthening their self-esteem. Think about what you will say (and how you will say it) to achieve that goal.

After the conversation, reflect on how it went. Do you think you made a positive impact? What can you learn from this experience?

My personal notes about respecting self-esteem needs

12 Clarify your communication objective

What does clarifying your communication objective mean?

Before you start communicating—regardless of whether it's in a live or virtual meeting, a one-to-one conversation with a team member, or a written message that you intend to send—think about the **purpose of the communication** first. Be clear about your communication objective and define what you want to achieve as a result of the interaction.

Why is clarifying your communication objective an important leadership skill?

People **expect clarity** from you as a leader—clarity about what you want, what your goals are, and what is expected of them. To avoid ambiguity in your communication, and to make sure that you are sending the right message (or that you will receive the right information that you need), always clarify what you want to accomplish before you start a conversation.

How do you clarify your communication objective?

Think about what you would like to achieve before starting any conversation, whether in oral or written form.

Here are some examples of the most common communication objectives in a leadership context:

- **Sharing information** (e.g. making sure that everyone in the team is informed about important current events in your organization).
- **Hearing different opinions** in a discussion of a particular problem (or getting different suggestions for how to solve it).
- **Decision making** (choosing the best possible option to solve a certain problem).
- **Influencing the emotional state of other people** (e.g. positively influencing the motivation of team members, or improving the team spirit).
- **Influencing actions** (e.g. helping team members change their behavior through giving feedback, or delegating a certain task).
- **Aligning the team** (making sure that team members understand the team's joint purpose and goals, and helping them to align their actions to achieve these goals).
- **Strengthening relationships** (building trust, both between you as a leader and team members as well as among your team).

In the case of meetings, you can state the objectives clearly up front in the meeting agenda (e.g. with agenda items being labeled as *information*, *discussion*, or *decision* items). In all other types of communication, make sure to also clarify your intentions up front: what do you want to happen as an outcome of your communication? What should the people you are communicating with know, think, feel, or do after the conversation with you?

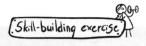

Clarifying your communication objective

Commit yourself to using a journal for one week, in which you quickly jot down your main communication objective(s) before you hold any important conversation.

Write down:

- what you want to happen as a result of the conversation, and
- what you will do to ensure that you will achieve this objective, taking into account the needs, interests and context of the people you are communicating with.

After one week, revisit your journal and reflect on how effective you were in achieving your communication objectives. What worked well (and why)? Where do you still see room for improvement? What could you do differently next time to ensure that you will be able to fully achieve your communication objectives?

My personal notes about clarifying my communication objective

13 Lead with questions

What does leading with questions mean?

Giving instructions makes people comply; **asking questions engages them**. Asking questions is much more than just a tool for receiving information. It is one of the most powerful ways to encourage participation, stimulate thinking and solve problems.

Why is leading with questions an important leadership skill?

When you think you know all the answers, you may be an expert but you are certainly not a leader. As a good leader, you will want your team to make progress—and there's no progress without asking new questions.

"**Our questions determine our thoughts,**" says the American coach and bestselling author Anthony Robbins, adding that successful people typically ask better questions, which then results in better answers.[3] When you are faced with a difficult situation, for example, it makes a huge difference whether you ask yourself a depressed *"Why me?"* or a powerful, forward-looking question like *"What can I learn from that?"* or *"What could I use it for?"*[4] Your questions will determine the direction of your thoughts and actions.

Nothing influences our focus of attention—and therefore also our behavior—more than the questions we ask. And that's not only true for our own mind, which we can positively influence with empowering questions, but also for our team.

When you ask questions, you are focusing the attention of your team members, and you stimulate their thinking. Asking good questions is a key step in every problem-solving process, and will help you create a culture in which responsibility for finding the right answers is shared in the team, rather than lying solely on your shoulders as a leader.

Including others in a problem-solving process rather than just imposing ready-made solutions sparks engagement and creates ownership in the team. It also encourages teamwork, as the right questions will set a joint process of inquiry in motion. And it will boost the self-esteem of team members, as they will feel listened to and valued for their contributions.

How do you effectively lead with questions?

The table below includes some examples of questions that you can use to create a positive, forward-looking, solution-oriented spirit in your team.

Question	Effect
"What do we want to achieve together in this project (and why)?"	Helps to get a joint view on the purpose and objectives of your teamwork
"What's great about this problem?"[5]	Focuses the team on positive thinking and fosters a learning mindset
"What would a perfect outcome look like?"	Helps to define an ideal future state
"What can we do to overcome this challenge?"	Focuses the team on potential solutions
"How can we improve this?", "What can we learn from this?"	Focuses the team on making progress
"What is working well in our team?", "What can we still improve?"	Helps the team to reflect on and improve the teamwork

Question	Effect
"What should we stop doing in order to improve things?"	Focuses the team on what not to do (which is often at least as important as what to do)
"What do you think about this?", *"Can I ask your opinion about this?"*	Shows your interest in another person's opinion and makes them feel included
"How are things going?", *"How was your weekend?"*	Shows that you care about the other person
"What can I do to help you succeed in your job?"	Improves collaboration, and shows that you care
"How can I be a better leader?"	Enhances your own leadership skills

Leading with questions

Next time you prepare for a one-to-one conversation with a team member or a meeting with your team, write down a list of the questions that you will ask.

My personal notes about leading with questions

14 Practice active listening

What does active listening mean?

Active listening means **paying undivided attention to another person with the aim of fully understanding the complete message they are trying to communicate.** If you are in an active listening mode, you will not just passively 'hear' what another person says. Instead, you will make an active effort to show interest, respond to what is being said, and comprehend not only the spoken word but also the underlying feelings and intentions. You will also refrain from interrupting and attending to your own thoughts when you are listening actively.

Why is active listening an important leadership skill?

We often pretend to listen while we are actually just focusing on what's going on in our own heads. As we think about how we want to reply, we fail to concentrate on what the other person really wants to tell us. We interrupt the speaker, finish their sentences, assess and criticize them, and are eager to present our own ideas and point of view (often disguised as 'good advice') instead of carefully paying attention.

Other people will usually notice when you just pretend to listen. If they sense that you are not listening, they will feel that you don't care about what they have to say, or—even worse—that you don't really care about them at all. That obviously won't help you to be seen as a respected leader.

When you are giving another person your **full and unbiased attention**, you can expect a very different outcome: they will feel heard, respected and understood. You will be able to build rapport and trust, and it will strengthen your relationship with them (as most people usually think very positively about interactions in which they really feel listened to). As an active listener, you will also help others better express themselves, thus increasing your chance of really understanding what they think and feel.

How active listening works

When you **listen actively**, you:

- Fully concentrate on what the speaker has to say.
- Pause your own thinking for a while.
- Refrain from interrupting and finishing sentences.
- Suspend judgment as you are trying to fully understand the other person.
- Show that you are paying attention (e.g. through looking at the speaker instead of glancing away, leaning slightly forward, and using encouraging words or gestures such as *"I see,"* a simple *"mm,"* or nodding to acknowledge what has been said).
- Ask clarifying questions and paraphrase in your own words to avoid misunderstandings (e.g. *"Did I understand this correctly?...,"* *"So you are saying that...?"*).
- Attend to nonverbal communication signals like body language and tone of voice (as people do not always explicitly say everything that they think and feel).

Becoming proficient in active listening demands conscious effort and a lot of practice. Once you master this essential communication skill, however, you will be rewarded with deeper conversations and stronger relationships.

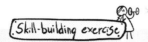

Practice active listening

Ask a person you trust (e.g. a friend or a colleague at work) to become your conversation partner. Explain to them that you would like to develop your listening skills.

- Ask your partner to talk about an issue that is currently very important for them.
- Try to just listen carefully and actively for a few minutes, keeping in mind all the aspects of active listening from above.
- Use questions and paraphrasing (repeating what was said in different words) to check whether you correctly understood everything and to clarify any misunderstandings.
- After finishing the conversation, discuss with your partner whether (and to what extent) they felt listened to and understood.
- Reflect on what was going on in your mind while you were listening.

My personal notes about active listening

_____

_____

_____

_____

_____

_____

15 Decode nonverbal signals

What does decoding nonverbal signals mean?

As human beings, we communicate at least as much with our body as with the spoken word, especially when it comes to expressing our emotions. Therefore, as a leader, in addition to listening carefully to what your team members say, you should also be able to **recognize and interpret what they tell you with their body language**. This will help you better understand other people's feelings and needs, and allow you to communicate more effectively.

Why is decoding nonverbal signals an important leadership skill?

Decoding nonverbal signals that other people are sending—as well as understanding what you convey to others with your own nonverbal signals—is a crucial communication skill. After all, communication is all about creating shared understanding, and that's difficult to achieve if you fail to understand what other people tell you with their tone of voice, movements, gestures, and facial expressions.

How decoding nonverbal signals works

Step one for becoming proficient in decoding nonverbal messages is **to notice them** in the first place. That's a task you deliberately need to focus on. Instead of just (passively) looking, you need to (actively) observe—to purposefully direct your attention to all the bodily expressions that others make, especially the seemingly 'small' ones.

This is followed by step two—**describing what you are noticing** (e.g. *"Chris is crossing her legs and turning her body away from me"*), and step three—**interpreting what you have observed** (e.g. *"Chris seems to be giving a signal that she does not like what I just said"*). Does a team member seem to be bored or engaged? Do they appear aggressive or calm? Are they in agreement with what has been said or do they seem to reject it?

Look for **nonverbal signals of comfort or discomfort** that will allow you to better assess how other people feel about certain issues. Joe Navarro, a former FBI agent and a renowned expert of nonverbal communication, describes a few relatively common nonverbal displays of discomfort: compressed lips, jaw shifting, rubbing the skin under the chin or on the neck, avoiding eye contact, or narrowing or covering the eyes.[6] These expressions send a completely different message than, for example, relaxed facial muscles, a slightly forward-leaning open body position, or an encouraging smile with eye contact, which are all signs of agreement and engagement.

Experienced communicators also know that body language can be ambiguous, and is potentially influenced by a person's cultural background. Therefore, in order to avoid misinterpretations, you should ideally **look for patterns** rather than just single expressions, as well as for congruence (e.g. in tone of voice, gestures and facial expressions) to be more confident in correctly interpreting the message that is being sent. Although nonverbal behavior does not necessarily reveal everything about other people, Joe Navarro recommends believing the body when you are in doubt. After all, we have all used body language much longer than the spoken language—both from an evolutionary point of view and in our own lives.[7]

Decoding nonverbal signals

For the next meeting that you will attend, give yourself the task of carefully observing and interpreting the nonverbal signals that other people around the table are sending.

- First, focus on **noticing the nonverbal signals**: which facial expressions, bodily movements or changes in tone of voice can you recognize when certain questions are asked or statements are made? What exactly do you observe?
- How do you **interpret these nonverbal signals**? Do they convey comfort or discomfort? Is there any other information that you can glean from people's bodily reactions (e.g. are people who are constantly confirming each other's opinions with nodding forming alliances on certain topics)?
- Is there a **congruence between words and bodily expressions**? If not, what could be the cause?
- What do the nonverbal signals tell you about the **interests, needs and feelings of your team members**? How could this information be useful for you as a leader?

My personal notes about decoding nonverbal signals

16 Present your ideas in a persuasive way

What does it mean to present your ideas in a persuasive way?

As a leader, you will often have to **present your ideas to others**. Ideally, you will be able to do so in a convincing way. Presenting persuasively means telling a compelling story, in which you (1) identify a concrete problem (and why it should matter to your audience), (2) raise an important question that needs to be answered, and (3) present your 'big idea' for how the problem could be solved, together with compelling reasons for why this is the right course of action.

Why is presenting your ideas in a persuasive way an important leadership skill?

When you communicate, you want to make an impact on others. You want them to understand an idea, change their attitude toward a certain issue, or act in a certain way. Presenting an idea in a persuasive way will help you achieve these communication objectives.

How do you present your ideas in a persuasive way?

There are two questions you should always keep in mind when planning a presentation:[8]

- **Who is the audience?** (What are their interests and expectations? What do they already know? What do they still need to know?)
- **What is your main message?** (The one 'big idea' that you would like to get across: what you would like your audience to know or do.)

Once you are clear about these two points, organize your presentation in the following way:[9]

1. **First, make sure you get the attention of the audience.** Describe the situation, and relate it to something that the audience cares about (e.g. *"I know we all care about creating a good learning experience for our students."*)

2. **Describe the problem:** what's not perfect about the current situation, and why should it matter to the team? (e.g. *"With the current seating arrangement in our classroom, it is very difficult to stimulate interaction between the students, which we all know is highly important for creating an engaging learning atmosphere."*)

3. **Clarify the question that needs to be answered.** As we discussed earlier, questions direct people's thoughts. Make sure to formulate a compelling, future-oriented question. Ask, for example, *"So what can we do to tackle this challenge?"* (or in our specific case, *"How can we improve the learning experience for our students?"*).

4. **Provide a persuasive response.** Present your one 'big idea' and explain why this will solve the problem. Use several arguments. Ideally, you will be able to provide three good reasons that support your idea (e.g. if your 'big idea' is to invest in new classroom furniture, the three reasons could include: *"It will create a highly interactive learning environment that will certainly contribute to better learning outcomes"*, *"We will be able to engage our students"*, and *"We will become much more attractive for new students when they see our innovative classroom setting"*).

Here are a few further suggestions from communication experts about how to present persuasively:[10]

- Use **vivid examples** (with 'real people doing real things')
- Use **metaphors** (e.g. *"With the new classroom, the atmosphere will no longer be like in a dreary office of endless cubicles. Instead, we will have a beautiful garden in which our students will be able to grow and thrive."*).
- Use **decisive language** (*"We must change ..."* instead of *"Maybe we should change ..."*)
- Maintain **eye contact** with your audience, **articulate clearly** (don't hurry, **take a breath,** and give your audience the **time to digest** what you said), and make good use of your **body language** (e.g. paint pictures with your hands).

Presenting ideas in a persuasive way

Before holding your next presentation or team briefing, write down the main message that you want to get across (in one sentence). Then prepare, in a few more sentences: (a) what you will do to get the attention of the audience, (b) the problem you will address, (c) the concrete question you will ask, and (d) your response to the question (the 'big idea' and three supporting arguments).

My personal notes about presenting ideas in a persuasive way

17 Speak to the heart

What does speaking to the heart mean?

Speaking to heart means communicating in a way that **engages the feelings of other people**, connecting with them not only cognitively but also emotionally.

Why is speaking to the heart an important leadership skill?

"It is necessary to have regard to the person whom we wish to persuade, of whom we must know the mind and the heart," wrote the French mathematician and philosopher Blaise Pascal in the 17th century.[11] Even earlier, in ancient Greece, Aristotle observed that there are three basic means of persuading other people: **ethos** (or appealing to ethics—persuasion based on the credibility and character of the leader), **logos** (or appealing to logic—persuasion based on convincing logical arguments), and **pathos** (or appealing to emotion—persuasion based on creating an emotional response in the audience).

Modern neuroscience confirms that our emotions strongly determine how we think and act. We will usually react very differently, for example, when we experience an emotional state of hope and passion than when we are paralyzed by anxiety and fear. If you really want to influence other people, you need to be able to use pathos and appeal to their emotions.

How do you speak to the heart?

There are two main categories of emotions:

- **Positive emotions** (e.g. hope, joy, passion, compassion, gratitude, or love)
- **Negative emotions** (e.g. anger, anxiety, fear, sadness, or frustration)

The words and metaphors that you use can have an impact on the emotions that are triggered in another person. "*We could all lose our jobs if we are unable to fix this problem*" will send a completely different emotional message to, for example, "*Let us be grateful about this opportunity to learn. How can we fix this problem in a way that will make us stronger?*" Use words with a positive emotional connotation to spark positive feelings, such as 'thankful,' 'winning,' 'trust,' 'enthusiastic,' 'passionate,' 'great,' or 'amazing.'

Another way of engaging the feelings of your audience is to **tell stories**—especially stories about people that your audience can identify with. Stories are emotional experiences, and the really good ones describe a transformation in which the 'hero' of the story is facing and overcoming a challenge.

The third path to persuading with pathos and speaking to the heart of others is to **speak *from* your own heart**. When you speak from the heart, you are completely authentic, genuine, and emotionally sincere. You are exposing your 'real self' and expressing your feelings. You are sharing your passions and hopes, but you are also openly communicating about your fears. It takes courage to express your feelings in this way, because you make yourself vulnerable. But as the American researcher and best-selling author Brené Brown says, vulnerability is all about "showing up and being seen."[12] You can't be a courageous leader—and you can't really reach the heart of other people—without having the courage to speak from your own heart.

Speaking to the heart

In your next conversation with a person that matters to you (e.g. a friend, family member, or good colleague), try to deliberately speak *from* the heart and *to* the heart:

- Before the conversation, think about the issue you would like to talk about. Listen inside yourself—which words or metaphors can best describe your own feelings about the issue? What do you *really* want to say to the other person?
- Enter the conversation with good intentions. Make sure that you want the best for the other person as well as for yourself.
- Before you speak, make sure that you are fully present. Take a breath. Then let the other person know how you truly feel about the issue you want to talk about.
- After the conversation, reflect on the impact of your mindful and open communication on both the other person and yourself.

My personal notes about speaking to the heart

18 Harness the power of feedback

What does it mean to harness the power of feedback?

Feedback is a form of communication in which you share information that can help another person improve their performance. It comes in two main categories: **positive feedback** (when you as a leader recognize a person's strengths, efforts and contributions) and **constructive critical feedback** (when you openly discuss what could be improved).

Why is giving feedback an important leadership skill?

Feedback is the fuel for making progress. As leadership expert Joseph Folkman says, "without feedback, we are flying blind."[13] Honest feedback gives your team members a great opportunity to reflect on their strengths and weaknesses, and to recognize the impact of their actions and behavior. It helps them to get a realistic self-assessment, provides them with a chance to learn and grow, and enables them to bring their performance to a higher level.

How do you harness the power of feedback?

The power of **positive feedback** is particularly easy to use: just open your mind to actively recognizing other people's strengths and contributions, and tell them how much you value them. Be as specific as possible, and explain exactly what you find great about what they do.

Stanford psychology professor Carol Dweck observed that it can be a lot more effective to **praise efforts instead of abilities** if you want to help other people grow.[14] For example, instead of saying *"You are the best presenter,"* you could say *"Wow, you must have put a lot of effort into creating this exceptional presentation."* That will reinforce the positive behavior, as you give the other person the feeling that their effort is seen and recognized. Praise feels incredibly good—when it comes from the heart!

So what about **constructive critical feedback** then? Well, that's a little more tricky, because it can potentially trigger very negative feelings. After all, no one really likes to be criticized. Just try to tell someone *"That was really a bad performance,"* *"You need to control your temper,"* or *"You must change yourself!"* and you will almost certainly get a negative reaction.

Giving critical feedback effectively does not mean telling another person what's wrong about them or their actions. It means entering into a **dialogue** about how things could be improved. It is much more important to ask the right questions and to listen well than to provide 'clever advice' in a patronizing way.

So here's how effective constructive feedback works:

1. Make sure you hold your feedback conversation **at the right moment** in time (ideally shortly after the event that you would like to give feedback about). The other person should also be in a stable emotional state that will allow them to process the feedback.
2. Share your observations **as objectively as possible**, without sounding accusatory (e.g. *"I have observed that you often come late for our morning meetings"*).
3. Ask **how the other person sees the situation** (e.g. *"What's your view on this?"*)—and then listen carefully.

4. Ask the other person **how they would like to tackle the issue** (e.g. *"So what could we do to improve the situation?"*). Let them make their own suggestions and commitment to improve instead of telling them what to do.

When you follow these four steps with the good intention of helping the other person, they will feel heard instead of being attacked. You will also increase the chance of getting real commitment to making a change rather than just compliance.

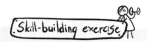

.Skill-building exercise

Harnessing the power of feedback

- **Exercise 1:** The next time one of your colleagues or team members does something well, make a note of it and in particular the specific attitudes or behaviors that you valued. Then find a way to make sure your colleague or team member receives this positive feedback from you.

- **Exercise 2:** The next time you need to give critical feedback to someone, take some time before the conversation to think about how you can frame it constructively. Think about how to open the conversation without sounding too accusatory or harsh (e.g. instead of saying *"Could I please have a word with you?"* try something like *"I really appreciate the work you've been doing on [specific project/ task]. I wanted to chat with you about how we could make some further improvements."*).[15]

My personal notes about harnessing the power of feedback

19 Master tough conversations

What does it mean to master tough conversations?

Leaders are sometimes confronted with tough conversations, where the **stakes are high**, there's **conflict** involved (i.e. people's opinions and interests clash), and **negative emotions** can be aroused.[16] Mastering these conversations means creating an atmosphere of dialogue in which all sides can openly share their thoughts and feelings with the aim of developing mutual understanding and shared meaning.

Why is mastering tough conversations an important leadership skill?

There are several types of tough conversations that leaders can face, for example:

- Giving critical feedback to a team member (see also *Skill 18 Harness the power of feedback*).
- One person (maybe you or another team member) being attacked in a conversation by someone else.

- Reminding a team member (or your boss) that they are not keeping their commitments (see *Skill 34 Ensure accountability*).
- Discussing a conflict between team members.
- Delivering bad news (e.g. giving notice to a team member).

These situations are unpleasant, but as much as we would want to avoid them, they are often necessary to enable progress in your team and organization. That's why it's highly important for you as a leader to competently master such conversations.

How do you master tough conversations?

Here are a few expert tips on how you can approach tough conversations as a leader:[17]

- First, always see them as a **dialogue**—as an opportunity for everyone to openly share all the necessary information, as well as their thoughts and feelings regarding the controversial issue. Dialogue means that you share your story, but at the same time invite the other person to share their own version of the story too. Ask questions first, and listen carefully to the answers (so that the other person feels understood—see *Skill 14 Practice active listening*).
- Try your best to make the conversation a **safe space**. People get emotional when they feel disrespected. And when they are emotionally aroused, they will be in a kind of 'fog' which will make it nearly impossible for them to communicate well. Therefore, try to be aware of how your words and actions can affect the self-esteem of others (see *Skill 11 Respect self-esteem needs*). Refrain from personal attacks, or blaming, humiliating or putting general labels on people (*"You are always such a ..."*), or failing to show respect, for example by interrupting others when they are speaking. Real masters of tough conversations are both "totally frank and completely respectful."[18]
- When you sense that you have violated respect and hurt the feelings of another person, **apologize** sincerely.

- Be **clear about your intentions.** You can, for example, use contrasts to make sure that you are not misunderstood—explain what you do not intend or mean first, and then clarify what you do mean instead.
- You do not need to make a decision in the conversation itself. Its primary purpose is to **improve mutual understanding** and **create shared meaning.** If possible, however, you can try to explore whether you can find a **mutual purpose** (is there a way to improve things for both sides?) and then brainstorm ideas and strategies that could help you achieve that mutual purpose.

The key for mastering tough conversations is to see them as a dialogue and to always keep the conversation respectful. Even if it's a tough issue to discuss, you can still show that you care about the other person.

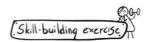

Preparing for a tough conversation

Before you hold your next tough conversation:

- Prepare a set of questions that you could ask to better understand the situation from the perspective of the other person.
- Try to think about a potential mutual purpose (*"What is important for all parties involved?"*) and what you could contribute to achieving it.

My personal notes about mastering tough conversations

20 Become a master negotiator

What does becoming a master negotiator mean?

A negotiation is a special form of communication. It's a **dialogue between people with different interests or intentions,** but with the clear aim of reaching an agreement. As a master negotiator, you will be able to prepare and conduct negotiations in a way that creates beneficial outcomes for all sides, while at the same time strengthening the relationship between the parties involved.

Why is being a master negotiator an important leadership skill?

There will hardly be one day without negotiations in your leadership role. You will have to negotiate to get resources for your team, negotiate the distribution of tasks, negotiate about salaries with or for your team members, negotiate with other departments, and likely also negotiate with customers, suppliers, or partners.

Developing your negotiation skills will help you to confidently manage any situation in which interests collide.

How do you become a master negotiator?

The key to becoming a master negotiator is to **be well prepared** for the negotiation. Experienced negotiators know that success is usually determined long before the real negotiation begins. Here's a short checklist with five key questions that you should always be able to answer before you enter into a negotiation:

1. **What is your BATNA?** That's negotiators' jargon for the 'best alternative to a negotiated agreement.' The better your best alternative (i.e. what you would do when you walk away from the negotiating table without a deal), the better your power position in the negotiation. It is therefore highly advisable to invest in the search for better alternatives (thus increasing your BATNA) before the negotiation.

2. **What do you have to offer the other party?** What makes you unique? What could your negotiating partner get from you that they can't get anywhere else?

3. **What are your priorities?** You will usually have a range of different points to negotiate. Define up front what is really most important for you (be crystal clear about your hierarchy of goals), and think about where you would be willing to make concessions in order to achieve your priorities.

4. **What are the other party's needs?** What will their priorities be, what motivates them, what are their aspirations, what fears could they have? What will most probably be their main requests, and what arguments and questions will they have? (You can even role-play with a friend or colleague for a perfect preparation.) Considering the other party's needs, where will you have common interests?

5. **What are the consequences of different outcomes of the negotiation, both for you and for the other party?** Think about which outcomes and consequences would be ideal for you, and which ones you would still be willing to accept.

Ideally, prepare yourself for the negotiation in written form. Create an outline with the main arguments that you will put forward and formulate the questions that you will ask.

Once you are well prepared, it's time to proceed with the actual negotiation:

- Start with a joint commitment to **negotiate for a mutually beneficial result**.
- Clearly **explain your own interests** (not only what you want, but also *why* you want it), and listen well to **fully understand the interests of the other party**.
- Instead of entrenching yourself in your own positions, **try to find solutions together that will serve the interests of both sides**. A good negotiation is a joint problem-solving process in which both sides win.

Go through the whole process with the right mindset. Stay focused on your priorities, and at the same time give your best to find a solution that is acceptable and beneficial for both sides.

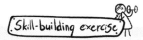

Preparing for your next negotiation

Before your next negotiation, go through the five key questions for preparing a negotiation above. Take your time to think about the answers. Write them down before you start negotiating.

My personal notes about becoming a master negotiator

Clarify purpose and priorities

. . . .

This chapter will enable you to:

» Determine your purpose, set goals, and develop strategies for your team.
» Clarify your priorities, discerning what's really important from what's not.
» Learn what and how to delegate.
» Apply a systematic approach to problem solving and decision making.
» Use your time wisely for the things that really matter.

People expect a leader to provide orientation and to set a direction—to lead them into a better future. "A leader is a dealer in hope," said Napoleon Bonaparte. Just think about it—would you want to follow someone who is telling you that there's no hope and things will only get worse in the future? We do not follow hesitaters and whiners; we follow people who are able to change things for the better. Creating a better future is what we need leaders for.

As a good leader, you've got to make sure that everyone in your team clearly understands three things (ideally in this order):

1. Your **purpose**—*why* what you do as a team is important.
2. Your **common goals**—*what* are you trying to accomplish together.
3. Your **priorities**—*how* you will get things done: your strategy as well as the key tasks and activities for fulfilling your purpose and reaching your goals together.

This chapter will help you develop the skills needed to define your team's (and your own) purpose, goals, strategy and priorities, so that everyone in your team (including you as a leader) will understand the value and importance of what you are doing, where you're heading toward, and how you will get there.

21 Have a clear purpose

What does having a clear purpose mean?

Everyone needs a 'why' for their work. Having a clear purpose means there's a **compelling reason for doing something**. It's an essential prerequisite for people to be motivated to put effort, energy, and enthusiasm into their work.

Above all, **purpose provides orientation**. It helps you to understand what you are here for—both as a leader and as a team. It defines your identity. And it reminds you of the impact you're making on the world.

Why is having a clear purpose an important leadership skill?

Having a sense of purpose gives **meaning** to your work. Research confirms that having a sense of purpose has a positive impact on work performance.[1] This is important both for you as a leader as well as for the team as a whole. Without a clear purpose, it is difficult—if not outright impossible—to ensure that a group of people works collaboratively in the right direction.

"The best teams invest a tremendous amount of time and effort exploring, shaping, and agreeing on a purpose that belongs to them both collectively and individually," write Jon R. Katzenbach and Douglas K. Smith, two leading experts on team performance, about the central role that 'purposing' plays for creating high-performance teams.[2]

A clear purpose does not only **ensure orientation** and **enhance motivation**, it will also **facilitate the prioritization of goals and tasks** (as people will understand which activities are really important to fulfill the purpose—see also *Skill 24 Set the right priorities*). It will also **improve collaboration**, as team members have a shared cause to work for.

How do you define a clear purpose for your team?

Don't try to 'invent' a purpose: try to discover it instead. A purpose only works well if it is authentic and sincere—if it is 'lived' rather than imposed. Take the following three steps to **discover your team purpose:**[3]

1. **Write down what your team does.** In a few sentences, describe the key activities of your team, as well as the products or services that it delivers (e.g. *"Our team runs the local university canteen. We prepare lunch for the people who work and study at the university."*)
2. **Clarify who are the main beneficiaries of the work of your team.** For whom is your work really important? Who would miss you the most if you're no longer completing your work? (e.g. *"Our work is really important for students and faculty members."*)
3. **Ask yourself why your work is so important for the beneficiaries.** Think about the final impact that your work has. Ask several 'whys.' For example: *"Our work is important because students and faculty members want to eat at lunchtime."* A second 'why' could reveal that *"They need to eat at lunchtime to keep their energy levels high in the afternoon,"* and a third 'why' that *"They will be able to learn better if their energy levels are high."*

Following these three steps, our university canteen team could, for example, come up with the following team purpose:

The purpose of our canteen team is to provide the students and staff of our university with a healthy lunch that allows them to have a better learning experience in the afternoon.

It is good practice for leaders to **involve their team in defining the team purpose,** for example by going through the three steps together or at least giving them the chance to review and discuss a first draft. After all, a purpose will only become fully effective if the team members view it as their common purpose.

Defining your purpose as a leader

Having a clear purpose is not only important for your team—it can also be extremely valuable for you as a leader. You can use **your personal leadership purpose** as a kind of 'inner compass' that guides you in your role as a leader.

Try to follow the same three steps from above for defining your personal purpose as a leader:

1. Think about your core tasks as a leader. What are you here for?
2. Clarify who are the main beneficiaries of your work as a leader (this will most probably include your team members).
3. Ask yourself what makes your work as a leader important for them. How and why do you make an impact as a leader? (Remember to use several 'whys.')

My personal notes about having a clear purpose

---

22 Think strategically

What does thinking strategically mean?

When you think strategically, you will take some time to reflect on (1) where you stand at the moment, (2) what the future will probably look like, (3) what unique value you and your team would like to create in the future, and (4) how you will make this possible.

As you will have noticed, strategic thinking goes beyond how we use the term 'strategy' in everyday language. It's not only about determining the steps that you will take to reach a certain goal (which is included in point (4) above), but more fundamentally about **finding and developing opportunities for creating value in the future**.

Why is strategic thinking an important leadership skill?

Strategic thinking has the following benefits:

- You **proactively create the future** you want for you and your team rather than just being carried along by external events.

- You will **develop a clear sense of direction** for your team. Your team members will better understand what you would like to achieve together and why.
- You will be able to **identify and exploit opportunities** that you might have missed without thinking strategically.
- You will **create the potential for success in the future** in a structured way.
- You will better **understand what you need to do today to continue to create value tomorrow.**

Strategic thinking is an essential activity for leaders who want to adapt to a changing environment and provide their team members with meaningful common goals.[4]

How do you think strategically?

You will need to reserve some time for thorough strategic thinking. Ideally, you will take some time off from your daily work to work on your strategy together with your team, maybe in the form of an off-site retreat. Many leaders also find it useful to hire an external strategy consultant for facilitating the strategy development process.

Strategy development basically revolves around asking and answering the following **five key strategic questions:**[5]

1. Where are we **now**? (Which strengths and weaknesses do we have?)
2. What will the **future** look like? (Which opportunities and threats can we see?)
3. Which **options** do we have for creating unique value in the future (in terms of the arena that we want to engage ourselves in and the value that we want to create there)?
4. Which of these options is **the best one** for ensuring the survival and thriving of our team (or organization) in the future? Where will we engage our efforts, and what unique value will we create there?
5. Which **concrete action steps** will we take to build the potential for being able to create that unique value in the future?

Especially for answering question 2 (which requires understanding key developments and trends in the environment), it can also make sense to include experts from outside of your team or organization in the process. They will provide you with new perspectives and ideas, and maybe open your eyes to new opportunities that you wouldn't have been able to see just within the team.

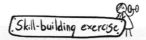

Thinking strategically with the 'From-To-How' framework

'From-To-How' is a simple yet powerful framework that will help you to communicate a strategy in a way that is easy to understand. Here's how it works (see also the example in the figure below):[6]

1. Identify a **core challenge** for your team or organization ('From').
2. Briefly describe the **desired future state** in which the challenge will be overcome ('To').
3. Derive and describe the **initiatives and actions** that will lead to the desired future state ('How').

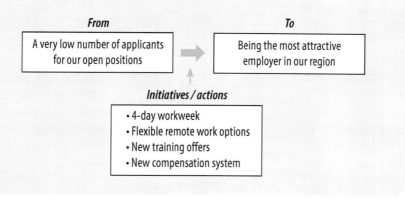

My personal notes about thinking strategically

23 Be clear on your goals

What does being clear on your goals mean?

It's your fundamental job as a leader to reach goals together with your team. Without common goals, there's no need for a leader.

Being clear on your goals means two things:

- First, **formulating the goals for your team in a clear and unambiguous way,** so that it is easy to determine whether you have achieved them or not.
- Second, **clearly communicating your joint goals** so that everyone in the team understands and ideally internalizes what you're aiming to achieve together.

Why is being clear on your goals an important leadership skill?

The term 'goal' can be defined as "the end toward which effort is directed."[7] That's exactly what you would like to achieve as a leader: making sure that the efforts of your team members are focused on reaching certain ends (and fulfilling your team's purpose—see *Skill 21 Have a clear purpose*).

Clear goals will help your team members understand what they should work on. When the goals are understood and accepted, they will create and sustain momentum in your team.

How can you be clear on your goals?

A widely known tool for formulating goals in a clear and unambiguous way is the **SMART** acronym. It stands for the five characteristics of clear goals. They should be:

- specific (with an exact definition of what should be accomplished),
- measurable (so that you can keep track of your goals and know to what extent you have achieved them),
- achievable (realistic),
- relevant (for fulfilling your purpose), and
- time-bound (with a clear deadline).

A smart way to formulate SMART goals is to **ask smart questions—** both of yourself and your team members:

- Does everyone clearly understand what we would like to accomplish together (and why)? [S]
- How will we know whether we have achieved the goal—and how will we measure progress? [M]
- Is everyone confident that the goal is achievable? And do we have all the necessary resources and competences in the team to make it happen? [A]
- Is the goal aligned with the team's overall purpose (and are we all committed to it)? [R]
- And what's the deadline for reaching our goal? [T]

Don't forget to always ask **who will be responsible and accountable** for reaching the goal, and who else will contribute to realizing it. Don't expect goals to be achieved without accountability (see *Skill 34 Ensure accountability*). Last but not least, keep in mind that you will usually get more commitment from people if you involve them in the goal-setting process than if you just impose a goal on them.

Setting your goals with the 'Pyramid Principle'

Use what McKinsey consultant Barbara Minto called the 'Pyramid Principle' to create a hierarchy of aligned goals for your team. Here's how it works (see also the example in the figure below):[8]

1. Start the pyramid of goals with the **most desirable outcome** (the most important goal you would like to achieve) at the top.
2. Ask yourself **what would need to be true for you to be able to achieve your most desirable outcome**. Use positive statements to formulate clear sub-goals.
3. Continue the process to a further level of **sub-goals** if necessary.

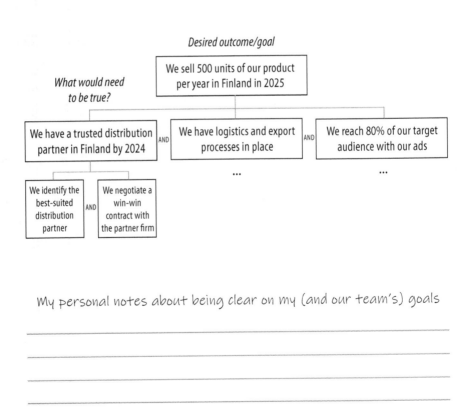

Desired outcome/goal

What would need to be true?

We sell 500 units of our product per year in Finland in 2025

We have a trusted distribution partner in Finland by 2024 **AND** We have logistics and export processes in place **AND** We reach 80% of our target audience with our ads

We identify the best-suited distribution partner **AND** We negotiate a win-win contract with the partner firm

...   ...

My personal notes about being clear on my (and our team's) goals

24 Set the right priorities

What does setting the right priorities mean?

Setting the right priorities is about discerning what is really important from what is not. The word **'priority'** stems from the Latin *prior*, which simply means 'first.' Setting priorities therefore means deciding on what comes first in the sense of what the important goals and tasks are—both for you as a leader and for your team as a whole.

Setting priorities also means **deciding what not to do**. "First things first," the famous management thinker Peter Drucker said, "and second things not at all."[9]

Why is setting the right priorities an important leadership skill?

Setting priorities helps to **focus your own and your team's efforts and energy on the really important goals and tasks**. Having a clear priority is like a lighthouse that prevents you from getting lost in the endless sea of 'urgent matters,' which is really just another way of describing things that are important for other people.[10]

Effective prioritizing means that you will **use your time and resources wisely**, for the things that really matter (see also *Skill 30 Use your time wisely*). It can bring more **direction, clarity and order** to the work and will also contribute to reducing stress levels (as team members know what to focus on when they are faced with competing demands).

How do you set the right priorities?

Here's how you can set the right priorities for yourself as a leader as well as for your team as a whole:

- **Focus on what is needed to fulfill your purpose.** Clarity of purpose (see *Skill 21 Have a clear purpose*) is a prerequisite for being able to prioritize. The answer to the question *"Which activity will contribute the most to fulfilling my/our purpose?"* will be the best guide toward your priorities. The less vague and more concrete your purpose, the easier it will be for you to identify the activities that you will need to undertake to achieve it.
- **Use clear criteria for distinguishing between what is important and what is not.** If you have different tasks or projects to choose from, you can use criteria like *impact* (in addition to how much it will contribute to fulfilling your purpose, you can also assess whether a task or project will help you follow your strategy and reach your main goals), *effort needed for implementation* (including team members' time, money, and other resources), *risks* involved, or *stakeholder interest* (how important is it for key stakeholders?).
- **Include your team members in setting priorities.** Most people are not very keen on simply being told what to do. Discussing potential priorities with your team members before a definite decision is reached will help you to get a higher level of commitment from your team.
- **Dare to say 'no.'** To prioritize effectively, we also need to "eliminate the nonessentials,"[11] which are all the things that do not help you fulfill your purpose and achieve your goals. Eliminating the nonessentials means having the courage to say 'no' to some or maybe even to a lot of requests. This is easier to implement if you politely state why you're saying no (e.g. because you are "already terribly over-

committed at the moment" or you "fully need to focus on project X"), and if you remind yourself that each time you're firmly saying no to something, you're also saying yes to what really matters (see also *Skill 29 Eliminate the nonessentials*).

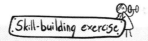

Setting your priorities with an I² matrix

Use a two-dimensional **I² matrix** for prioritizing different tasks, projects or initiatives (I² stands for *impact* and *implementation*):[12]

1. Assess the tasks, projects or initiatives in terms of their potential impact (e.g. on a simple scale of *high*, *medium* and *low impact*).
2. Estimate how much effort will be needed to implement the tasks, projects or initiatives (e.g. on a scale of *easy*, *somewhat difficult* and *difficult to implement*).
3. Make the tasks, projects or initiatives in the upper left corner (*high impact* and *easy to implement*) your priorities.

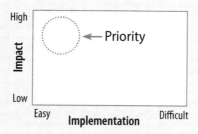

My personal notes about setting the right priorities

25 Delegate with impact

What does delegating with impact mean?

The root of the word 'delegating' lies in the Latin *delegare*, which means "to transfer or entrust something to someone." When you delegate, you **transfer a task to someone else** (usually a team member) and trust that they will be able to complete this task. Delegating will be particularly effective if (a) the task is completed in the right quality at the right time, and (b) it's an opportunity for those who are completing the task to learn and grow.

Why is delegating with impact an important leadership skill?

A lot of managers feel stressed by the plethora of open tasks they need to complete. This is often a sign of an inability to delegate. Several reasons can lead to this problem: they might have a lack of confidence (or trust) in the abilities of their team members; they might fear burdening their team members with too much; they may believe that no one could perform this task as well as they can; or they could have an inner desire to be seen as an effective problem solver or decision maker.

Whatever the underlying reason, if you are not able to delegate effectively, you will run into troubles as a leader. You will end up with a huge pile of work and team members who are demotivated by the feeling that you don't trust them, and you won't be able to use the full power of your team. In short: you will become highly inefficient in your work.

Effective delegation will **free up time for your priorities**—for the activities that really count—and it can also be a great tool for engaging your team members and providing them with opportunities to develop themselves.

How do you delegate with impact?

Effective delegation includes the following three tasks:

1. Identify **the right person** to delegate to.
2. Hold an effective **assignment meeting** and gain commitment.
3. Don't forget to **follow up**.

First, **identify the right person for a task**. Many leaders will just think of those who they see as 'best suited' for the task. Of course, choosing people with the right skills will raise the chance of getting the best possible outcome. But it can also lead to work overload for the high performers in the team, and may prevent other team members from learning something new. A good alternative is to **choose a team member for whom the task could be a great learning opportunity**. In this case, you will not only motivate your team members with new, challenging tasks, but can also use the delegation process as a systematic way of improving the competency base of your whole team.

If you have found the right person to delegate to, it's time for step 2: **making the assignment**. In the assignment meeting with your team member, make sure to:

- clearly define the **expected outcome** (and the deadline),
- provide information about **why the task is important** (its purpose),
- clarify which **resources and support** are available,
- agree on how you will **monitor progress** together, and
- get a **clear commitment from your team member** to take responsibility for completing the task.[13]

The assignment meeting shouldn't just be a monologue in which you 'instruct' another person on what they have to do. Ideally, it's "a **dialogue** in which two people gain a common understanding of what needs to be done and why."[14]

Step 3 is to **follow up**. Just assigning a task to someone doesn't automatically mean that it is also done. Make sure to get in touch with your team member again to discuss progress, and to give them feedback on their performance (see *Skill 18 Harness the power of feedback*).[15]

Determine what you should delegate

As a leader, you will ideally spend your time on the tasks with the highest possible impact, and delegate the other tasks to your team members. Take the following steps to determine which tasks to delegate:[16]

1. Compile a list of all activities that you spend your work time on.
2. From the list you compiled for point 1, highlight those activities that you are capable of performing much better than others.
3. Then highlight (with a different color) those activities that create the most value for your team and/or organization.
4. Identify those activities that you highlighted in both points 2 and 3. These are the ones to best focus your energy on.
5. For the other tasks on your list, think about who you could delegate them to.

My personal notes about delegating with impact

_____

_____

_____

_____

26 Solve problems

What does it mean to solve problems?

Problems are situations that are being perceived as "unsatisfactory and difficult to deal with."[17] Problem solving is the process of **addressing these unsatisfactory situations** in a way that allows your team to overcome the obstacles and reach a joint goal.

Why is problem solving an important leadership skill?

We're living in a complex world in which change is the only constant. "Complex situations involve a number of 'wicked problems,'" writes Daniel Pittino, author of *The Concise Leadership Textbook*, adding that such problems "can be solved only through proper leadership."[18] With the term **'wicked problems,'** he refers to problems in which neither the causes are clear in the beginning, nor are there predefined solutions for how to deal with them.

Unlike simple problems that can be solved through applying tried-and-tested procedures and rules, wicked problems can only be solved in a collaborative problem-solving effort under the guidance of a leader. Pittino therefore concludes that "leadership effectiveness can be ultimately assessed by the ability to work with wicked problems."[19] In other words: the existence of wicked problems is why we need leadership—the ability to exert social influence to reach a common goal.

How do you solve problems together with your team?

A systematic problem-solving process includes the following five steps (also known as the '5Cs' of problem solving):[20]

1. **Clarify—make sure you're solving the right problem.** Before finding the right answer, you must first ask the right question. Try to clearly define which problem you're solving, ideally in written form (e.g. *"The problem is that..."*). Then make sure that you clearly understand the goals that you want to achieve, as well as the goals of others who are also involved in the problem situation.

2. **Causes—make the right diagnosis.** Step 2 is to gather data about the problem situation to identify the root cause (or causes) of the problem. A good doctor would never prescribe a therapy without having made a thorough diagnosis. As a leader, you should follow this good practice too.

3. **Create—find promising solutions.** Once you've understood the causes of a problem (or at least have a good idea about what they could be), it's time to collect ideas on how the problem could be solved. A good way of finding promising solutions is to ask others who have overcome a similar problem situation before. Don't be shy to ask for help! You can also brainstorm potential solutions together with your team, or use idea-generation techniques like logic trees or mind maps (see my book *Solve It! The Mindset and Tools of Smart Problem Solvers* for more details about how to find promising solutions for your problems).

4. **Choose—decide on the optimal solution.** When you've found several potentially promising solutions, weigh the pros and cons of each and choose the option that brings you closest to your goals. The I^2 matrix (see the skill-building exercise in *Skill 24 Set the right priorities*) could help you to find the solution with the highest impact and ease of implementation.

5. **Commit—make it happen.** Once you've identified your favorite solution, it's time to take action. Translate your idea for solving the problem into concrete action steps for you and your team members. If it's a bigger initiative, set up a project plan. Get the commitment of others who you need to make things happen, and start implementing your plan (and don't forget to make progress reviews along the way).

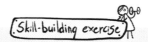

Use smart brainstorming for problem solving

Brainstorming is an idea-generation technique in which a group of people share ideas about potential solutions for a problem without judging each other. A frequently occurring issue in 'normal' brainstorming sessions is that some people tend to dominate the room, while others (usually more introverted team members) don't feel comfortable and contribute less than they actually could. **'Smart' brainstorming** tries to overcome this problem by taking the following four steps:[21]

1. Let the team members work individually on potential solutions first.
2. Then let them discuss their ideas in small groups.
3. Take a break (which is important to let the ideas sink in).
4. Only then start a group discussion in which you ask everyone to contribute and build on each others' ideas.

My personal notes about problem solving

27 Make better decisions

What does making better decisions mean?

Making a decision means **deliberately choosing what to do and what not to do**. Decision making is necessary in situations that involve trade-offs, where it's not possible to attain all goals of all involved parties. After all, if there was one option that could achieve all the goals, then you wouldn't really need to decide. Making a decision therefore always means deciding *against* something (or someone), which is one reason why some people are often reluctant to make decisions.

In addition to trade-offs, real decisions also involve a certain degree of **uncertainty**, meaning there are some factors involved that you cannot control but that will affect the eventual outcome. The existence of trade-offs and uncertainty means that better decisions are not necessarily those that lead to the 'perfect' outcomes (as the outcomes are also determined by external factors that are beyond your control). **Better decisions** are those which (a) are made deliberately and thoughtfully, (b) take into account all relevant information (from the perspective of all parties involved), and (c) can be clearly explained to others.[22]

Why is better decision making an important leadership skill?

Your team members will expect you as a leader to make decisions, especially the hard ones. As a leader, you need to set direction, and distinguish the essential from the nonessential. You might play it safe with indecisiveness, but it can ultimately ruin your credibility as a leader. Would you want to follow someone who never knows which direction to take?

But most team members will also be wary of people who just decide things without first trying to fully understand the facts or carefully consider the different options, and who are unable to clearly communicate why they are convinced that a certain path is the best one. In short: if you want to create trust with your team, strive for making better decisions.

How can you make better decisions?

Here's a simple yet powerful version of a deliberate and thoughtful decision-making process:

1. **Be clear on your goals.** What do want to want to achieve for your team? What do others want to achieve? As there are often trade-offs involved, it can make sense to rank the goals from the most to the least important one.
2. **Consider your options.** What alternatives do you have? For each option, you can then then assess (e.g. on a scale of '+' to '+++' and '−' to '−−−') how it will help (or hinder) you in achieving your most important goals. Make sure to include all relevant information in creating and assessing your options—especially the perspective of other parties that are involved in or affected by the decision.
3. **Choose the option that brings you closest to your goals.** If in doubt, always opt for the option that is best for the whole team or organization rather than for a single person or party (including you).

If you follow this simple three-step process, you will be able to explain to others the rationale of why you have taken your decision. Where there's a lot at stake, you will also want to carefully investigate the **risks** involved in each option as well as the **critical uncertainties** (those factors which are outside your control but can have an impact on the eventual outcome) before eventually making your decision.

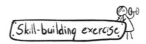

A template for making better decisions

The next time you have to make a decision, use the template below to get a better overview of your options. The goals and evaluations from '+' to '+++' and '−' to '−−−' are just examples that you will have to adapt to your own situation.

Goals »	Possible return on investment	Accepted by stake- holders	Fast to implement	Low risk	Total
Option 1	+	+	++	−	4+ vs. 1−
Option 2	+++	−−	−−	+	4+ vs. 4−
Option 3	++	++	−	++	6+ vs. 1−

In this case, option 3 seems to be the best one, with 6 plus points and only 1 minus point. You will then also need to consider the relative importance of the goals. Option 3 looks particularly promising if speed of implementation is not so crucial. If it is, however, you might also consider option 1 as an alternative.

My personal notes about making better decisions

_____

_____

_____

_____

_____

_____

_____

28 Identify the bottleneck

What does it mean to identify the bottleneck?

A simple definition of a bottleneck is a **congestion in a system**—a congestion that slows progress. In a production system, it's usually the point in the workflow with the lowest capacity. Work piles up at this point, and slows down the whole process. In project management, the bottleneck is a work stage that stalls or even stops subsequent tasks. In an organization, it's the most limiting factor that holds the organization back from achieving its full potential.

Identifying the bottleneck means **finding the key factor which limits the performance of the whole system**. Once you've found it, you can make it a priority to deal with the bottleneck, which will usually make a big difference to the productivity and performance of your team.

Why is identifying the bottleneck an important leadership skill?

Bottlenecks are the reason why projects get delayed, costs pile up, information flows are interrupted, and your team members become frustrated because they are unable to reach their full potential. Identifying and dealing with a bottleneck will help you to overcome these problems. When bottlenecks are unblocked, it will give your team the feeling of making progress. This will not only positively affect the performance but also the motivation of your team.

How do you identify bottlenecks?

In general, we can distinguish between **two types of bottlenecks**:

1. Bottlenecks that are caused by performance problems.
2. Bottlenecks that are inherent in the system.

'Type 1' bottlenecks (those caused by performance problems) occur when one or several team members do not deliver their work at the right time and/or in the right quality, thus slowing down or limiting the performance of all others who depend on the output of their work. Take a look at *Skills 34 Ensure accountability* and *47 Address performance problems* for ideas on how to deal with such a performance-based bottleneck (keeping in mind that the problem is not necessarily 'bad work,' but could also lie in a lack of resources or in a certain function being understaffed).

'Type 2' bottlenecks (those that lie 'in the system') can be more tricky to detect. They occur when individual team members all give their best, but there are other factors (for example, inefficient workflows, unclear role distribution and communication structures, a lack of data, or detrimental aspects of the organizational culture) which hold the team back from reaching its full performance potential.

So how can you **locate bottlenecks** then? One way is to look for typical symptoms of a bottleneck: long wait times for a certain output that is needed to make progress, work that is piling up somewhere, or high stress and frustration levels in particular parts of your team. If you want to be more systematic in finding the bottleneck, try to use techniques for visualizing a system. One example is a **process flowchart** in which you draw in sequential order the tasks that need to be completed to create a certain outcome. You can then use this flowchart to locate where bottleneck-related problems occur (e.g. through measuring the cycle time/delays at each step, or identifying where there are queues or frustrated team members). You can also use the 'Pyramid Principle' (see the skill-building exercise in *Skill 23 Be clear on your goals*) to define an optimal outcome of a particular system and draw a pyramid of factors that contribute to that outcome. Then try to find the factor which deviates the most from an ideal state in that pyramid, which is a potential candidate for being a bottleneck.

Once you have identified the bottleneck in your system, use your problem-solving skills (see *Skill 26 Solve problems*) to deal with it. Potential **ways of dealing with a bottleneck** are adding resources (maybe having more people work on it), reducing the strain on the bottleneck (e.g. making sure that the work arrives 'in perfect shape' before it reaches the bottleneck), or finding another way to process the work at the bottleneck (e.g. to digitalize a step in the workflow).[23]

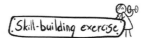

Identifying the bottleneck

Go through the following steps to identify and deal with a bottleneck in any system that you're observing:

1. Define the key outcome of the system.
2. Visualize the activities needed to achieve the outcome.
3. Locate the activity which is causing the most problems (in terms of congestion, e.g. long wait times, work piled up, stressed team members).
4. Find a way to deal with this bottleneck activity.
5. Circle back to point 3 (because whenever you have successfully dealt with one bottleneck, there's always another one to contend with).

My personal notes about identifying the bottleneck

29 Eliminate the nonessentials

What does eliminiating the nonessentials mean?

Learning to eliminate the nonessentials is important for **maintaining focus in your work**. When you have defined priorities for yourself and your team (see *Skill 24 Set the right priorities*), you need to protect them against the less important things that always come your way.

There are two strategies that you can follow here:

1. Not taking on new non-priority tasks (i.e. saying 'no' to new requests).
2. Deliberately eliminating unimportant tasks that you're already engaged in.

Strategy 2 is what we mean by 'eliminating the nonessentials' here. It's about **actively reducing the number of less important existing tasks and commitments** to create more space for the really important things.

Why is eliminating the nonessentials an important leadership skill?

As a good leader, you will always want to improve whatever you're responsible for (e.g. the products and services that your team provides, or the structures, processes, and systems of your organization). Many leaders are unfortunately conditioned to think that the best way of making improvements is to add something new. They start new projects and initiatives, and this helps to show how 'active' they are as a leader. However, such an approach of relentless adding will often end in disaster. It will likely lead to work overload and exhaustion in your team. And maybe you will even feel like you've become stuck in a never-ending rat race.

In addition to setting the right **priorities**, therefore, you need to be able to set the right **posteriorities**: the things you should *not* do any more. Systematically tidying up the clutter of nonessentials will help you and your team to focus on the essentials again—the tasks and initiatives that enable you to reach your big goals and fulfill your real purpose.

How do you elimit the nonessentials?

Management expert Fredmund Malik proposed the following approach to avoid what he called "ending up swamped in the garbage of needless activity":[24]

- On a regular basis (at least once a year), hold a **team meeting with the sole purpose of discussing and deciding on what you should get rid of.**
- In this meeting, ask the following questions: *"Which of our activities add the least value?", "Taking a look at what we are doing at the moment, what would we not start again today?", "What should we stop doing?"*

Many rules, procedures, forms, reports, meetings, or other activities—maybe even products or services that you're currently offering or customers you're serving—may have made perfect sense at the time when they were introduced. In a fast-changing world, however, it's advisable to take a look at them again and honestly assess whether they might have become outdated or useless in the meantime.

The American leadership author Michael Hyatt also recommends **filtering your commitments** from time to time, to 'prune away' the nonessentials. That could be a 'yes' that you've said too fast to a request requiring you to do something that you're not really passionate about, that is not really in line with your core purpose, or that you maybe don't even have the right skills and strengths for. Although Hyatt also emphasizes that "people of integrity keep their word," he says that you can still attempt to negotiate yourself out of an existing commitment in the following way:[25]

- First, make it clear that you would be willing to still hold your commitment if necessary.
- Explain why it wouldn't be the best outcome for the other party if you keep your commitment.
- Help them to find an alternative solution.

You could, for example, try a few sentences like *"Thank you once again for inviting me to this committee, but now I realize that it was a mistake to join. I feel that I can't really add much value here because... Would you be willing to release me of this responsibility if I help you to find someone who would be able to add more expertise to this committee?"*[26]

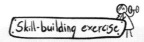

Eliminating the nonessentials

At the end of the work week, list all the activities that you've been engaged in during the week. Use the questions *"Which of these activities add the least value?"* and *"Which activities would I not start again today?"* to identify two or three nonessentials. Then prepare a plan of steps you will take to eliminate these unimportant activities in future.

My personal notes about eliminating the nonessentials

_____

_____

_____

_____

_____

30 Use your time wisely

What does using your time wisely mean?

Let's face it—in a leadership role, you will never have time for everything you want to do. That's why you need to deliberately choose what to do (and what not to do) in the limited time that is available to you.

Using your time wisely means **only doing things that really count**—being focused on the priorities that will help you and your team to fulfill your purpose and reach your goals. The skills that you have already learned in this chapter—from defining your purpose, goals and priorities to identifying bottlenecks and eliminating the nonessentials—will help you to better distinguish the activities that really matter (and that you should spend your time on) from those that add less value. Let us now add a few practical methods that will allow you to better manage (and therefore more wisely use) your time.

Why is using your time wisely an important leadership skill?

If you are able to manage your time well, you will be able to get the important things done. You'll be more likely to reach your goals when you spend more of your time on activities that help you achieve those goals. And you will also be less stressed when you're feeling in control of how you spend your time.

How do you use your time wisely?

Using your time wisely means **reserving most of your work time for activities that are linked to fulfilling your purpose and reaching your most important goals.** Becoming proficient in the other skills that we've already discussed in this chapter (e.g. defining a purpose, goal-setting, prioritization) is a major prerequisite for making this happen. Once you're clear about your priorities, you can use the following three simple methods to ensure that you will spend your time working on getting the really important things done:[27]

- **Focus on one big thing at a time.** Instead of having too many things to do at the same time, try to serialize—make one really essential project your number one priority and work on it regularly (every day!) until you have completed it. Then—and only then—start working on the next big project. In this way, you will save the switching costs that occur whenever you need to immerse yourself into a new task. It will also be very motivating for you and your team to see how you're making progress on an important project every day (see also *Skill 37 Create an agile team* about organizing your teamwork in focused 'sprints').
- **Work with two to-do lists.** The first to-do list is an 'open' one on which you can note down everything that you need or would like to do. Its purpose is just to get things out of your head. Once a to-do item is on paper, you no longer have to keep it at the top of your mind. The 'open' list can be very long. The second ('closed') to-do list should be very short. It contains a fixed number of really important to-do items (ideally no more than five). These are the ones that you will be working on. You may transfer the next most important item from your 'open' list to the 'closed' one only when you have successfully completed one item from your 'closed' list. Be aware that you will never be able to complete all the tasks on the 'open' list, but that's completely fine, as the two-lists system will always force you to spend your time on the really important things.

- **Take your time to organize your time.** Regularly reserving some time to reflect on your priorities—both as a leader and as a team— is an investment that will always pay off. Michael Hyatt, for example, suggests a weekly preview meeting with yourself (e.g. on Friday afternoon) in which you spend 30 minutes reviewing the previous week (including your learnings and biggest wins), take a look at your 'open' to-do list, and decide on your priorities and 'closed' to-do list for the new week. For further tips about how to use your reflection time well, see *Skills 10 Make self-reflection a habit* and *49 Organize reflective sessions.*

Using your time wisely

Set an hour aside and make sure you are undisturbed. Follow these three steps to plan how you will use your time wisely during the next four weeks:

1. Think about which (two to three) activities are the most important ones for fulfilling your purpose and achieving your main goals.
2. Schedule these priority activities into your calendar for the next four weeks. Make sure to reserve enough time for each activity (build in some slack here).
3. Schedule a 'meeting with yourself' once per week to review the progress you're making on your priority tasks.

My personal notes about using my time wisely

Build a winning team

This chapter will enable you to:

» Take the right steps to build an agile, high-performing team with a great team spirit.
» Create and maintain trust, rapport, and accountability in your team.
» Recognize the specific requirements of leading a virtual team.
» Manage conflicts in your team.
» Build your extended team through effective networking.

Talent wins games, but teamwork and intelligence win champion-ships,"[1] said basketball superstar Michael Jordan. This is not only true in sports, but for teams in any domain. As an intelligent leader, you will know how to unleash the power that lies in effective teamwork.

There's no doubt that it can be a considerable advantage to have tal-ented people in your team. The first skill of this chapter (*Get the right people into your team*) will address this issue. But then it's all about how team members interact and collaborate with each other, as well as with you as a leader.

In a **winning team**, you will find team members who know what they are responsible for (and feel accountable for it), a high level of trust, pro-ductive interactions (especially in team meetings), good personal rela-tionships, a constructive way of dealing with conflicts, and a strong com-mitment from everyone toward the team and its goals. The skills from this chapter will enable you to make all of this happen in your team too.

In addition, you will also find some tips about leading virtual teams, creating agile teams, and using clever networking strategies to nurture your 'extended' team of people who can support you in fulfilling your purpose and achieving your goals as a team.

31 Get the right people into your team

What does it mean to get the right people into your team?

According to a Gallup leadership survey, one of the most important pre-requisites for leaders to be effective is to "surround themselves with the right people."[2] Selecting the right people for your team means finding and recruiting those who **combine the right skillset with the right attitudes**.

That's certainly not an easy task, but one of the most important ones in your role as a leader. There is no other choice that influences your chances of success as much as choosing the right people for your team.

Why is getting the right people an important leadership skill?

A team can only be as good as the sum of its team members. The quality of the individuals in your team—combined with their willingness and ability to collaborate with each other—will largely determine the quality of the outcomes that you will be able to achieve as a leader.

Getting the right people on board will not only have a big impact on the results that you will be able to achieve with your team. It can also:

- **Save you time** (when new team members have the right qualifications, they will need less training).
- **Increase productivity** (as they bring in new skills that will enable them to assist the existing team with completing their tasks).
- **Boost team morale** (when they bring vital new skills and experience into the team, and provide support and encouragement for other team members).
- **Spare you a lot of money and effort** (which you would have to invest in finding a replacement if a candidate turned out to be the wrong one).

In short, your life as a leader will be much easier if you have the right people around you. After all, good people will do good work, and that will allow you as a leader to focus more on your leadership role instead of immersing yourself too much in operative details.

How do you get the right people into your team?

Take the following steps to get the right people on board:[3]

1. **Create a clear job profile.** Clearly define the main tasks and responsibilities. Use this as the basis for identifying key requirements that a potential candidate for the job should fulfill. Include qualification and skills requirements as well as personal characteristics that are needed for the job and for being a valuable member of the team (e.g. attitudes, personality, interpersonal skills, motivation, diligence).
2. **Search for suitable candidates.** In addition to posting a job ad, hiring a recruiting agency, or searching for candidates on professional social media networks like LinkedIn, you might also think about asking team members or other trusted people for referrals. Don't shy away from investing time and effort here—without a pool of suitable candidates to select from, you won't be able to get a suitable new team member.
3. **Select the best person for your team.** The selection process usually begins with screening résumés, in which your main task is to look for a good match with the key requirements for the job. Then it's time to interview the most promising candidates and check refer-

ences (an important step which is too often neglected). Rather than only conducting a formal interview where you ask questions and the candidate answers them, consider other ways you could get to know them better or test the skills they'll really need in the job. For example, ask them to give a presentation or role-play a certain scenario, or give them a tour around the building or take them for a coffee, and then notice how they interact with other people. Think about how you can actually test the skills you're looking for.

Think about **including other team members in the selection process**, particularly in the job interviews. After all, a good personal fit with the team is a major prerequisite for becoming a valuable new team member

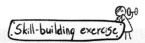

Add some creativity to the job interview

Most job interviews follow the same boring choreography (with questions like *"Why did you want to apply for this job?"*, *"Where do you see yourself in three years' time?"*, or *"What are your biggest weaknesses?"*). It's all predictable, and the candidates have already prepared their answers. Chances are high that you will hear that their biggest weakness is either 'being impatient' or 'being a perfectionist.'

Try to be a bit more creative to find out more about the real person behind the well-prepared interview façade. Compile a list of 'unusual' questions which can help you truly understand the other person (examples include asking them about the qualities that they admire the most in their parents, the biggest misperceptions that others have about them, or the book that had the strongest influence on their life).[4]

My personal notes about getting the best people into my team

_____

_____

32 Clarify roles and rules

What does clarifying roles and rules mean?

To create a high-performing team, you need to (a) **effectively combine the complementary skills** of team members and (b) make sure that they **collaborate in a coordinated way**. To make this possible, everyone in the team first needs to understand both their own role and the roles of the other team members. Everyone should know what they are expected to contribute and what they are responsible for.

Team coordination is another key task of a leader. It's about ensuring that the activities of the team members are well-synchronized. A simple way of ensuring well-coordinated work is to agree on a few rules that clarify how you are going to work together as a team.

Why is clarifying roles and rules an important leadership skill?

Teamwork means combining the skills of your team members to achieve something together that you (and the others) wouldn't have been able to achieve individually. Obviously, this will work a lot better if you are able to combine your skills in a coordinated way.

Clear roles and rules are two basic cornerstones of effective coordination. If everyone knows what they are responsible for and how they are supposed to collaborate with each other, it will be much easier for your team to work toward a common goal in a coherent way.

How do you clarify roles and rules?

There are two different types of roles in a team:

- Roles that are based on **professional skills and experience** (e.g. the market research specialist, the spreadsheet wizard, or the technical expert).
- **Team roles**: certain types of behaviors that people tend to show in a team setting.

Team roles could include, for example, a 'coordinator' (someone who takes care of organizing and coordinating the work), a 'teamworker' (takes care of the well-being of team members), a 'resource investigator' (focuses on helping the team get access to resources and information from outside), or a 'completer-finisher' (attends to the details and tries to make sure that project deliverables are completed thoroughly and without errors).[5]

Effective teams typically include **a diverse mix of both types of roles**–those based on professional expertise and team roles. It's your task as a team leader to ensure that you have the right mix of people in your team, and that all the necessary roles are adequately filled.

Teamwork will also become much easier if everyone knows their own role and the roles of others. Set aside enough time, therefore, at the beginning as well as during the teamwork to **clarify roles and expectations**. This includes finding answers to questions like:

- Who is responsible for what in our team?
- What expectations do you as a leader and the other team members have of each team member?
- What will each team member contribute to the team success?

In addition to clear roles, teams need clear rules. This is not about setting up endless documents with bureaucratic guidelines (that would quickly kill commitment in the team), but about agreeing on **a few ground rules** for how you would like to work together. That could include, for example:

- Basic rules of collaboration (e.g. regarding attendance, confidentiality, or accountability).
- How to communicate within the team.
- How decisions are made (see *Skill 27 Make better decisions*).
- How to deal with conflicts (see *Skill 38 Manage conflicts*).

It is good practice to discuss and agree on the ground rules when the team is newly formed, although it definitely makes sense from time to time to reflect together in your team whether the rules and routines of working together are still suitable and practical.

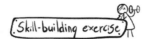

Reflecting on the team process

Schedule a reflection meeting for your team in which you discuss the quality of your team processes, with a special focus on the clarity of roles and rules of coordination. Ask the following questions in the meeting:[6]

- Are we clearly focused on our main goals and purpose in our team-work?
- Does everyone know who is responsible for what?
- What are our team norms or ground rules—and are they helping us to perform well (or do we need to change anything in our approach to working together)?
- Are the team processes perceived as being fair?

My personal notes about clarifying roles and rules

33 Establish trust and rapport

What does establishing trust and rapport mean?

Trust is the belief that other people are honest and reliable, and that they hold good intentions. **Rapport** is a friendly and harmonious relationship in which both sides feel safe openly expressing their feelings, and interact in a way that shows care for and understanding of one another.

Trust and rapport are strongly related to each other, and they are both important ingredients of ensuring team success. As a leader of a team, your focus should not only lie on 'getting the work done,' but also on building good relationships within the team—relationships that are based on trust and rapport.

Why is establishing trust and rapport an important leadership skill?

Imagine leading a team in which team members have established neither trust nor rapport with each other. You can expect a lack of open communication and limited information sharing in such a team. Team members will probably fear that others will take advantage of them, and will play it safe and cover their own backs instead of helping each other succeed. That's not the type of environment in which you will be able to reach high performance levels.

Researchers have observed significant **positive effects of trust on knowledge sharing and team performance**.[7] Team members who trust each other are more likely to share information and ideas, give each other honest feedback, and help each other with solving problems. Higher levels of trust and rapport will make your team stronger and more cohesive, which is particularly important when you are going through more challenging times.

How do you establish trust and rapport?

As a leader, you can try out the following strategies for fostering trust and rapport in your team:[8]

- **Create shared experiences.** Trust and rapport are developed over time when people get to know each other better on a personal level. Shared positive experiences play a crucial role here. Socializing at lunch or after work, attending seminars or conferences together, or celebrating success—these are all opportunities for creating stronger bonds within your team.
- **Encourage open conversations.** You can do so, for example, by being open and honest yourself (such as admitting your own mistakes or that you don't know something), inviting others to share both successes and challenges, and always objectively assessing both the benefits and the downsides of proposals together.
- **Avoid the blame game.** "Nothing kills trust quicker than blame," writes Michael Timms in a *Fast Company* article.[9] Instead of asking *"Whose fault is it?"*, take a solution-focused approach and ask *"What can we learn from this?"* or *"What could we change in our processes to avoid such a problem in future?"*.
- **Ensure accountability.** Trust is built when team members keep their commitments and promises, and when they know they can rely on each other. See *Skill 34 Ensure accountability* for more.
- **Discourage clique-building.** When a few team members interact very closely with each other (including on a personal level), it can

make others feel left out. Openly addressing such 'in-group' versus 'out-group' situations and using a different mix of team members in different projects can help to alleviate such problems.

Encouraging everyone in your team to **be open and honest in giving feedback** to one another is another way of building trust and rapport among team members (see *Skill 18 Harness the power of feedback*).

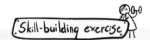

An activity for building trust and rapport in your team

Team retreats—one or a few days in which the team gathers off-site—are a great way of strengthening personal relationships between team members. Non-work activities are at least as important as work-related activities during such events.

In your next team retreat, set aside some time for every team member (including yourself) to present within a short time limit (e.g. three to five minutes) their answers to the following two questions:

1. What do I consider to be my biggest success during the last year (and what were the reasons for that success)?
2. What do I consider to be my biggest mistake during the last year (and what did I learn from making that mistake)?

This exercise will help your team members build more trust in each other, as it opens up a safe space for 'admitting' mistakes, which can also set the tone for further open conversations.

My personal notes about building trust and rapport in my team

_____
_____
_____
_____

34 Ensure accountability

What does ensuring accountability mean?

Accountability is all about **keeping commitments**. Ensuring accountability means that you as a leader are keeping your own commitments and promises toward others, while at the same time creating an environment which encourages all other team members to keep their commitments and promises too.

Why is ensuring accountability an important leadership skill?

Ensuring accountability is an important leadership skill because of all the **negative effects** that occur when people fail to keep their commitments and violate their promises:

- Work doesn't get finished at the right time and with the right quality.
- A high level of disappointment and frustration on the part of those who are not getting the input that they need from others to complete their own work.
- A higher level of conflict and a lower level of trust within the team.

- Negative effects on morale and team spirit.
- Negative feelings toward you as a leader as someone who isn't able to create an environment in which people act in a responsible way.

As a leader, it's your job to achieve goals and get things done together with your team. This is not possible without ensuring that everyone delivers the work outputs that they are supposed to deliver, i.e. without ensuring accountability. In teams where people hold each other accountable, there's a much higher chance of reaching **higher levels of trust, productivity, and employee satisfaction.**[10]

How can you ensure accountability in your team

There are five main points to consider for ensuring a high level of accountability within your team:

1. **Keep your own promises.** It all starts with your own behavior as a leader. Others will notice right away if you fail to keep your own commitments. And they will follow suit. You are setting the standards as a leader, and you can't demand from others what you are not able to deliver yourself.
2. **Define clearly what people are accountable for.** You can't feel accountable and act in a responsible way if you don't know exactly what you are accountable for. Make sure, therefore, that the expectations for your team members are clearly defined, and that they really understand what they are responsible for (get feedback from them on how they understand their responsibility; letting them explain what they are accountable for themselves can have a much stronger effect than you telling them what they should do).
3. **Agree on the consequences of violating commitments beforehand.** When you and your team members agree on accountability standards and consequences for those who violate their commitments at the beginning of a project (e.g. whoever doesn't deliver their work on time buys a round of pizzas for the others), the stakes are still low, as there is no immediate conflict situation yet. It will, however, make it much easier for you to address accountability issues later in the process (and you may even get a pizza for free).

4. **Hold accountability conversations.** Follow up on commitments that have been made. If a commitment is broken by a team member (especially on an issue that is important), then address it in a personal conversation with them. Enter into a dialogue about why the commitment was not fulfilled and what could be done to ensure that future commitments will be kept (see also *Skill 18 Harness the power of feedback*).

5. **Recognize responsible behavior.** It's not enough to only discuss deviating behavior. Don't forget to also recognize and praise those who are keeping their commitments. Saying thank you for holding commitments (in private and in public) can work wonders too.

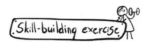

Holding accountability conversations

Next time you hold an accountability conversation, consider the following tips proposed by Kerry Patterson and his colleagues in their book *Crucial Accountability*:[11]

- Apply the **CPR model**: in the first conversation, focus on the content (C) by discussing what went wrong; in a second conversation (if the accountability problem persists), focus on the pattern (P), i.e. on what has happened over time; if a third conversation is necessary, focus on what it all means for the relationship (R).

- Create a safe environment at the start of the conversation, share your observations, then ask a 'diagnostic question' (e.g. *"What happened from your point of view?"*). Listen to their response, respond to the problem, and make a plan together of how and by when to resolve it.

My personal notes about ensuring accountability

_____

_____

_____

35 Make meetings productive

What does making meetings productive mean?

Teams spend a lot of time in meetings (and arguably too much time when it is not used productively). Making meetings productive means that they have a **clear purpose**, the **right people** are invited (only those who can make a contribution), the participants come to the meeting **well-prepared**, there is a **clear focus** on accomplishing the purpose of the meeting, and everyone knows exactly what their **next tasks** are when they leave the room (and when these tasks need to be completed by).

Why is making meetings productive an important leadership skill?

Meetings can be a great tool for coordinating team effort. But they can also be a real nuisance, especially when they are badly prepared and badly run. Some meetings are nothing more than endless discussions, in which people who like to hear themselves talk bore those who have better things to do. As this is probably not the type of meeting that you want for your team, it pays to put some effort into planning and running a meeting in a more effective way.

How do you make meetings productive?

There are some simple rules for holding an effective meeting:[12]

- Define a **clear purpose** for the meeting (e.g. disseminating information, brainstorming potential solutions for a problem, decision making, or distributing work tasks).
- Only **invite participants who can really contribute** to accomplishing the purpose of the meeting.
- Make sure **someone is in charge of running the meeting** (this could be you as the leader or someone else; they could take on the role of 'moderator' or 'meeting chairperson').
- Distribute an **agenda** before the meeting (including information on the objective of each agenda item, e.g. giving information, generating ideas, or making a decision) so that everyone who is invited can come well-prepared.
- **Respect the time of others**—do not run over the agreed finishing time.
- **Invite everyone to contribute** (as you hopefully only invited people who have something to contribute to the meeting in the first place).
- **Make clear decisions** (especially on who does what).
- **Write the decisions down** in short meeting minutes and include a **'next steps' list** (including clear responsibilities and deadlines for the action items).
- Make sure to **circulate the meeting minutes** to all participants after the meeting.
- Do not forget to **follow up**—review the 'next steps' list and call on people when their work is due.

Before inviting others to a meeting, always ask yourself **if the meeting is really necessary at all**. The best way to achieve more productive meetings is to not start them at all if they are not really needed and if there's a more efficient and effective way of achieving a certain purpose.

Analyze your next meeting

Next time you are participating in a team meeting, try to use it as an opportunity to analyze its effectiveness and productivity. Ask yourself the following questions:

- Did the meeting have a clear agenda? Was the agenda distributed to the participants beforehand so that you and your colleagues could prepare yourselves well for the meeting?
- Was the purpose of the meeting clearly communicated?
- Did the meeting moderator ensure that the discussion stayed focused on the agenda items?
- Were the right people invited? Were they all able to contribute?
- Did the meeting result in a clear action plan? Did everyone know what their tasks are and by when they need to complete them?
- What else did you notice that contributed to making the meeting productive?
- What could be organized differently to make the next meeting more productive?

In addition to self-reflection, you could also use these questions to discuss the productivity of your meetings together with your team (e.g. at the end of your next team meeting).

My personal notes about making meetings (more) productive

36 Lead a virtual team

What does it mean to lead a virtual team?

A **virtual team** (also called a **remote team**) is a geographically dispersed group of people who are collaborating with the help of digital tools. Leading a virtual team means leading from a distance, and includes both focusing the team on accomplishing the common purpose and encouraging positive collaboration in the virtual working space.

Why is leading a virtual team an important leadership skill?

The Covid-19 pandemic has led to an unprecedented rise in remote work. People have got used to working from home and communicating with their colleagues through digital platforms and tools. Leading a virtual team has therefore become a key competence for leaders in almost all types of organizations.

Remote teamwork poses new challenges for leaders, including a lack of personal interaction (which is really important for creating trusting working relationships), working across different time zones, technological barriers (e.g. bandwidth problems), the difficulty of creating and maintaining a team spirit despite a lack of face-to-face encounters, and a higher probability of miscommunication as nonverbal communication signals are much more difficult to convey and decipher over electronic communication channels.

When a team is dispersed, the leader's role of orchestrating goal-oriented teamwork becomes even more important for ensuring that the virtual team can accomplish its purpose.

How do you lead a virtual team?

Here are a few tips for leading a virtual team:[13]

- **Establish and repeatedly emphasize clear team norms.** This includes, for example, *attendance rules* (e.g. no multitasking during meetings, or rules for cameras being switched on or off in video-conference meetings), *communication rules* (e.g. not interrupting each other), *task completion standards* (e.g. who is to be informed in what way when someone is running late on a task), or *reporting rules* (who reports what to whom at what time).
- **Create a dedicated space for informal communication.** You could, for example, organize a group in a messaging app in which team members can share informal messages, schedule 'coffee calls' with the sole purpose of having an informal chat (and drinking a coffee together), or reserve a few minutes at the beginning or the end of a team call for giving team members the opportunity to connect on a more personal level with a bit of small talk.
- **Ensure clarity in communication.** Making your own expectations clear is as important here as careful active listening (see *Skill 14 Practice active listening*). It is also advisable to ask for clarification before making premature assumptions about what others think or mean.
- **Establish a personal connection with team members.** It's even more important than in on-site teams, where you can regularly hold a quick chat in the coffee corner, to provide team members with an opportunity to express individual concerns as well as to recognize personal performance in one-to-one meetings.

- **Keep meetings short and crisp.** Try to keep team meetings within 40–45 minutes (or even shorter) if possible. If you need to work on one topic for a longer time period, use breakout groups, surveys, or other forms of engagement to combat screen fatigue.
- **Encourage collaboration.** Instead of letting everyone grow lonely behind their computer screens at home, consider encouraging team members to work in (changing) pairs on certain issues, thus providing them with an opportunity to connect with and learn from each other.
- **Organize offline get-togethers.** However well you are leading your virtual team, holding a few face-to-face meetings from time to time (or, even better, team bonding events outside of the work context) can contribute a lot to building interpersonal trust and fostering team cohesion.

Last but not least, don't forget to **celebrate success** together in your virtual team (e.g. ask your team members to come with their favorite drink to the next remote meeting and toast to the success of a team member or the team as a whole). Make sure that people get the feeling that the team is accomplishing something together.

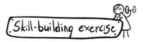

The five ground rules for your virtual team

Do you already have a set of official team norms for your team? If not, try to organize a team meeting in which you discuss which five ground rules you could set yourself as a team in order to be able to productively and effectively work together. Make sure that everyone has a voice in the discussion and agrees with the outcome.

My personal notes about leading a virtual team

37 Create an agile team

What does creating an agile team mean?

In a fast-changing environment, you need to be able to quickly react and adapt to new challenges. An **agile team** is a self-organized team that is perfectly suited to work in such a fast-paced environment. Instead of following a strict plan, an agile team works in smaller chunks and in close collaboration among themselves as well as with their 'clients' (the users of the team's output). Agile teams usually work **iteratively,** i.e. the work is first completed in a 'rough' form (or as a 'prototype') and then refined in repeated cycle.

The agile way of working originates from the field of software development. Due to its effectiveness in dynamic environments, it has become a widespread method for organizing teamwork in other domains too.

Why is creating an agile team an important leadership skill?

There are a number of benefits that come from an agile way of working:

- **Speed**—agile teams can quickly address new challenges.
- **Motivation**—progress is fast and visible.

- **Flexibility**—priorities can be adjusted in a flexible way to adapt to changing situations.
- **Involvement**—clients (and potentially other stakeholders) are involved early on in the process, which helps to create trust.
- **Transparency**—due to frequent feedback cycles, both team members and clients always know where the team stands.

How do you create an agile team?

The following general guidelines can help you develop an agile team:[14]

- Encourage **self-organization** in the team and allow 'local leaders' to address challenges as and where they arise.
- Work with a **'test-and-learn' mindset**, in which the team uses short 'sprints' (short periods of work, e.g. two weeks, in which team members focus intensely on accomplishing one priority task) to try to solve a problem, then get in touch with each other and important stakeholders to get feedback, learn from it, and improve.
- Ensure **short-term accountability**, with frequent feedback meetings (e.g. short daily stand-ups or sprint review meetings at the end of every sprint, which can be used to assess progress, distribute tasks, and keep the team oriented toward reaching the goal.

The team can also use **agile methods** to accomplish their goals. One of the most widely used agile methods is called '**scrum**.' It is a framework for collaborating as an agile team and includes:[15]

- The definition of certain **scrum team roles**, including the *scrum master* (a person who understands the scrum system and is focused on improving the team processes), the *product owner* (the person who is accountable for getting a certain goal accomplished) and the *developers* (everyone else in the scrum team).
- A few **scrum artifacts** that provide information about the team's tasks and progress, including a *product backlog* (with all the tasks that need to be completed in the overall project), a *sprint backlog* (a plan for what is to be achieved in a particular sprint), and *increments* (concretely defined action steps that need to be completed within a sprint).

- Regular **scrum events** that take place in a scrum project, including the *sprint planning meeting*, daily 15-minute *scrum meetings* to jointly review progress, a *sprint review* to check the outcomes at the end of each sprint, and a *sprint retrospective* in which the team discusses what went well in the sprint and what could be improved next time (similar to the reflective sessions in *Skill 49 Organize reflective sessions*).

Regular scrum events can help to speed up decision making and improve communication in a way that renders other meetings unnecessary.

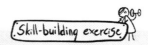

Planning an agile sprint for your team

Here's how you can **organize a sprint planning meeting** for an agile team:[16]

1. Agree on a **sprint goal** in your team (What would you like to achieve with a sprint and for whom and how will this sprint add value?)
2. Let the team members select **items from the product backlog** (the overall list of tasks that need to be completed in a project) to be included in the current sprint. Try to estimate what is possible to accomplish within a limited timeframe.
3. Let the team members **define their work packages** (called *increments* in scrum terminology) and how they plan to deliver them (in a way that defines when the work package can be considered 'done,' i.e. is successfully completed)
4. Include the 'why' (sprint goal), 'what' (product backlog items), and 'how' (increments) in a **sprint backlog**, a visual roadmap of all that needs to be done to successfully complete a sprint.

My personal notes about creating an agile team

_____

_____

38 Manage conflicts

What does it mean to manage conflicts?

A conflict is a situation in which people or groups of people have opposing needs or different opinions. Whatever you call it—a controversy, a struggle, a clash, a fight—it's always a situation that is unsatisfactory for the parties involved.

For a leader, managing conflicts means being able to **identify conflict situations early** and then apply an adequate strategy to resolve the conflict, in a way that **minimizes negative outcomes** and **maximizes the chance of creating positive outcomes** for all the parties involved.

Why is managing conflicts an important leadership skill?

If they are not managed well, conflicts can have a whole range of **detrimental effects** on individuals, teams, and organizations. They consume a lot of time and energy (that could otherwise be used for productive work) and can trigger a spiral of negative emotions that can cause psychological problems. This can result in low morale, increased stress levels, a decrease in productivity, absenteeism, or even members leaving the team.

On the other hand, if a conflict is handled effectively, it can potentially also have **positive effects**. It can teach people to take other perspectives into account, help to create new, innovative ideas and solutions, provide opportunities for practicing communication skills and becoming more resilient, or even lead to a better level of understanding and trust among the parties involved if they are able to resolve the conflict together.

How do you effectively manage conflicts?

There are four steps that you as a leader can take to manage a conflict situation:[17]

1. **Try to prevent conflicts before they arise.** When you make decisions, distribute tasks and resources, or communicate with your team, think about whether there are potential triggers for conflict (e.g. perceptions of being treated in an unfair way, poor coordination, or a competition for scarce resources). In this case, try to prepare a strategy for mitigating potential negative impacts up front, e.g. by trying to help team members who are affected by a decision understand the decision process and implications in one-to-one meetings before you publicly announce your decision. Another way of preventing conflicts is to develop clear guidelines and codes of conduct that will help avoid behaviors that could potentially lead to conflicts. A third strategy to prevent conflicts is to reduce interaction between people who are likely to come into conflict with each other (e.g. by physically separating their workplaces).
2. **Remain calm and neutral in conflict situations.** First of all, you do not need to involve yourself in all conflicts. If it's a minor issue, you might well let those involved sort it out for themselves, as long as it does not have any negative effects on the overall team climate or performance. If you sense that it is necessary for you to intervene, try to clearly communicate with all parties involved that you are not going to take sides, but will help them find a solution that considers their interests but above all the interests of the team and organization as a whole.
3. **Understand the parties' goals and work collaboratively to find a solution.** Identify the underlying interests of each party (not only

their current position regarding the disputed issue, but also their underlying motives, e.g. being fairly treated or reliably getting input for their own work). Once you've reached a common understanding about what is important for each party, try to take a solution-focused approach (instead of playing the blame game). Brainstorm solutions that could be beneficial or at least acceptable for all parties involved.

4. **Keep an 'unsolvable' conflict under control.** If you are unable to reach a solution that is acceptable for all sides, try one of the following strategies for at least preventing the conflict from having severe negative effects on the whole team: (a) separate the opponents (minimize overlaps in their work), (b) clarify the rules of interaction between the opponents, (c) change the conditions that trigger the conflict (e.g. refrain from paying out those bonuses that used to lead to conflict within the team), or (d) offer professional mediation and/or personal counseling support to help those who are involved in the conflict better cope with the situation.

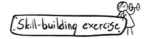

Develop a conflict management process with your team

Try to develop a conflict management process together with your team. Agree on which steps you will take when a conflict occurs. Team members who are taking part in such an exercise will then usually be more likely to show commitment to following the agreed procedure once an actual conflict arises.

My personal notes about managing conflicts

39 Create and maintain a team spirit

What does it mean to create and maintain a team spirit?

Team spirit is an **emotional commitment** that team members show toward the team. It means that team members are proud to be part of the team, and that they are engaged and motivated to give their best to help other team members—and the team as a whole—succeed.

Team spirit is created both on an **individual level** (manifested in the willingness to trust and help others in the team) and on a **group level** (where a group identity and shared commitment to a cause is formed).[18]

Why is creating a team spirit an important leadership skill?

Research results indicate that there are **strong links between the degree of trust between team members, team cohesion, and the performance and success of teams.** Such relationships have been found in various team settings, for example in sports teams or global virtual teams.[19]

Without a team spirit, teams tend to split up into an 'in-group' (those with better relationships among themselves and with the leaders) and an 'out-group' (those with lower-quality relationships with the leader and other team members), which can lead to a range of detrimental effects, including higher stress levels or 'out-group' members becoming disloyal to the team, or even engaging in disruptive behaviors.[20]

It is one of the main responsibilities of a team leader to create and maintain a positive team spirit and avoid falling into the 'in-group' versus 'out-group' trap.

How do you create and maintain a team spirit

Here are a few tips for what leaders can do to foster team spirit:[21]

- **Bring the right people into the team.** Obviously, it is much easier to develop a team spirit with team players than with sociopaths. It is therefore advisable to check during the recruitment process if newcomers bring the right attitude and energy to the team (see *Skill 31 Get the right people into your team*).
- **Invest enough time in 'purposing':** clarifying the team's common purpose and goals together with the team members.
- **Make sure that the team roles and functions are clearly defined and accepted by all team members**, so that everyone knows how they (and others in team) can best contribute to the team's success.
- **Develop an efficient way of collaborating within the team** (including efficient meeting procedures—see *Skill 35 Make meetings productive*).
- **Keep an eye on the relationships between team members.** Try to spot emerging conflicts early, and manage conflicts so they do not escalate and have a negative effect on the team climate (see *Skill 38 Manage conflicts*).
- **Give everyone the feeling of being valued and included.** Give everyone a voice when discussing important matters. Try to reflect regularly on whether there are people with an 'out-group' feeling, and ensure they are adequately recognized by you as a leader and included in team activities.
- **Engage in team-building activities.** Reserve some time in which you deliberately focus on fostering relationships and building camaraderie between team members, for example in off-site meetings or joint activities outside of the immediate work context.

- **Celebrate success and learnings.** Achieving something together can be a real booster for the team spirit, especially when you celebrate your success together too. But you can also focus on maintaining team spirit in more difficult situations, for example through discussing—and then also 'celebrating'—the learnings that the team takes away from a failure. After all, tomorrow's success is always based on what we're learning today.

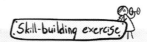

Celebrate your team's learnings from failure

If something didn't work out as planned for your team, get together and try to discuss the following two questions:

- What are our main learnings from the failure?
- What will we do differently next time to raise our chances of success?

Try to adhere to the following guidelines for the discussion:

1. We have one goal—to learn how to improve our team performance.
2. We do not blame anyone or anything (not even the circumstances).
3. We do not focus on what is wrong, but on what we can improve.

When you have agreed on your learnings, celebrate them with your team (e.g. by having an after-work drink together). Remember that your team's learnings—and the positive spirit with which you go through both good and bad times together in your team—are the seeds of future success.

My personal notes about creating and maintaining a team spirit

_____

_____

_____

40 Cultivate your extended team

What does it mean to cultivate your extended team?

Cultivating your extended team means building and maintaining a **supportive network**. These are the people who—in addition to your team members—help you achieve your goals through providing information, resources, and other types of support that you need. In order to be able to make use of your network, you first need to build and nurture it through **networking activities**, in which you invest in creating good relationships.

Why is networking an important leadership skill?

In a leadership role, you will often need the help of other people to accomplish something. This will, of course, include the members of your immediate team. But on many issues, you will also need outside support. A well-functioning network can provide you with valuable information and contacts, answers to open questions, advice on how to solve a problem, and access to resources (and sometimes new career opportunities too).

Nurturing your network will also help you to raise your profile as a leader, as **people typically regard those who have a strong network as more powerful**. Power is often defined as the capacity to influence others—and that will become a lot easier if you are able to enlist the support of other influential people in your network.

How do you become an effective networker?

Here are a few steps that you can take to build and extend your supportive network:[22]

1. **Clarify what you would like to achieve.** Once you know your goals (see *Skill 23 Be clear on your goals*), think about what kind of support you will need to be able to achieve these goals.
2. **Define your 'target network.'** Who are the people (both inside and outside of your organization) who you either depend on or who could provide the type of support that you will need to reach your goals? Try, in particular, to identify the influential and 'powerful' people in your domain.
3. **Establish relationships with the people in your target network.** Try to actively contact the people on your target list. You could, for example, help or support them on something that is important for them, congratulate them on an achievement, or ask them for advice on an important matter. Using existing contacts as a bridge to establish new relationships will increase your chances of building these new relationships.
4. **Take part in networking events.** Conferences, fairs, training programs, and other types of events in which people in your domain meet are great opportunities to extend your network. Most people who attend such events will also be willing to start a conversation with you, even if they don't know you yet.
5. **Use professional social media networks.** You can use online networks like LinkedIn to get in touch and interact with people in your target network and present yourself as an attractive new network partner.
6. **Nurture your network.** Provide valuable input for your network partners, either through sharing relevant information, helping them

connect with each other, or just sending positive and encouraging messages (e.g. congratulating them on their birthdays or on job changes). A well-nurtured network will be one of the greatest assets that you possess as a leader.

Drawing your supportive network

Step 1: Take a piece of paper and draw a circle with your name in it in the middle of the page. Then think about the key people in your existing network. For each one, draw a circle with their name in it. The distance between your circle and the circle of a network partner should indicate the importance of the person for achieving your personal and professional goals.

Step 2: Once you have placed the network partners in circles on the page, draw a line from each network partner circle to your own. Use a thick line for a strong relationship, and a thin line if the relationship is rather weak.

Step 3: Take a look at the resulting picture and think about who you need to strengthen your relationship with. Write down what you could and will do to invest in your relationship with these people.

My personal notes about cultivating my extended team

Help others grow

This chapter will enable you to:

» Create opportunities for your team members to learn and grow.
» Develop coaching skills and help others realize their full potential.
» Help your team members develop the right attitudes and skills to perform well in their jobs (and address performance problems if they should arise).
» Manage change processes effectively.
» Become a role model in developing both yourself and your team.

There are two major yardsticks for your success as a leader: first, the degree to which you are able to fulfill your purpose as a team (see Chapter 3); and second, the impact that you're making on your team members or 'followers.' You can only claim to be really successful in your leadership role if you're **helping your team members grow**—if they feel that through working with you, they're getting the **opportunity to develop themselves both personally and professionally**.

This chapter will enable you to upgrade your **people development skills**. You will learn how to recognize your team members' strengths; how to then provide them with the right challenges, coaching support, and development opportunities to build on those strengths; and how to encourage them to continually show a high level of engagement. We will also take a look at how to deal with performance problems and how to grow as a whole team through well-managed change processes.

You cannot demand that others develop themselves, however, without being willing to constantly work on your own personal growth as a leader. That's why the last two skills in this book will focus on reflection and developing yourself as a leader. After all, as John F. Kennedy knew, "leadership and learning are indispensable to each other."[1]

41 Recognize their strengths

What does recognizing their strengths mean?

Recognizing the strengths of your team members means deliberately trying to find out which kind of tasks they are able to perform particularly
well. It will enable you as a leader to **match tasks with strengths**, which
will allow both individual team members and the team as a whole to
achieve higher performance levels.

Why is recognizing strengths an important leadership skill?

Understanding your team members' strengths will enable you to intel-
ligently make use of them. You can provide them with tasks which are
tailored to their strengths, and on which they therefore have a chance to
perform exceptionally well. Or you can bring different strengths together
in a team, which will allow you to tackle complex and challenging tasks
for which a variety of different strengths are needed.

In addition to **improving performance**, strengths-based leadership
can also have a strong **motivational effect**. Researchers at Gallup have
interviewed over 10,000 people about the most important traits of leaders. They found that when leaders focus on their followers' strengths, the

chance that the followers will be engaged increases eightfold.[2] Tom Rath, a member of the Gallup research team, therefore considers uncovering team members' strengths to be the "most critical part" of a leader's job.[3]

If you know their strengths, you can also provide your team members with development opportunities for improving their strengths even further and becoming top-class in their domain. People usually thrive when they work in a field that matches their strengths, and giving them the chance to build their strengths to an even higher level can have a much stronger motivational effect than focusing on offsetting weaknesses.

Recognizing the strengths of others is therefore one of the most important strengths of an effective leader.

How do you recognize your team member's strengths?

Recognizing strengths actually has two meanings:

1. First, it means that you are able to **understand which abilities people have** that allow them to consistently perform strongly in a certain activity.[4]
2. And second, it means that you are **recognizing the person for their strength**, by showing them how much you appreciate it. This type of recognition is also one way of reinforcing the use of a strength.

So how can you recognize a strength of a team member in the sense of the first point above? There are a few strategies that you can use here:

- Think about which tasks and activities your team member has performed exceptionally well in. Which underlying strengths could have contributed to their outstanding performance?
- Think about what you could learn from your team member.
- Organize team feedback rounds in which team members give feedback on the strengths that they see in each other.
- Use (paid) assessment tools that can help uncover the main strengths that your team members have (for example, Gallup's *CliftonStrengths* assessment tool).

To learn how to appreciate your team members' strengths, see *Skill 18 Harness the power of feedback.*

Recognizing your team members' strengths

Invite a team member to take a look at the following table and ask them to draw a circle around the five terms that they think best describe their main strengths (they can add additional terms if they cannot identify their main strengths on this list).

Ability to concentrate	Dependability	Kindness	Risk taking
Ability to delegate	Detail orientation	Leadership ability	Self-confidence
Ability to take criticism	Determination	Mental balance	Self-control
Accuracy	Diligence	Open-mindedness	Self-initiative
Adaptability	Discipline	Organizational skills	Self-motivation
Analytical thinking	Eagerness to learn	Patience	Social intelligence
Articulateness	Enthusiasm	Perseverance	Spontaneity
Assertiveness	Flexibility	Persuasiveness	Strategic thinking
Commitment	Good listener	Positivity	Tactfulness
Communication skills	Good networker	Prudence	Teaching skills
Creativity	Good presenter	Reliability	Team player
Critical thinking	Humor	Resilience	Trustworthiness
Curiosity	Innovativeness	Responsibility	Willingness to learn
_____	_____	_____	_____
_____	_____	_____	_____

Then organize a 'strengths discussion meeting' in which you discuss the strengths together with the team member. Try to identify together which types of tasks are the 'best fit' for your team member's strengths.[5]

42 Create a fear-free environment

What does creating a fear-free environment mean?

Living and working in a **fear-free environment** is a basic prerequisite for people to be able to grow and thrive. It means that

- people can **speak up freely** without having to fear being repri-manded or rejected,
- they **do not have to fear negative consequences** when taking a risk and potentially making a mistake, and
- they are **neither bullied nor exposed to any kind of behavior that humiliates them.**

Why is creating a fear-free environment an important leadership skill?

A team of researchers took a look at more than 180 teams at Google to find out which factors make a team effective. The most important fac-tor that they found by far in highly successful teams was **psychological safety**: the extent to which team members felt that it was safe for them "to take risks and be vulnerable in front of each other"[6]

This is fully in line with the results of over 20 years of research by Harvard Business School professor Amy Edmondson, who in her book *The Fearless Organization* also identifies psychological safety as a major factor that explains performance differences in teams and organizations.[7] Psychological safety, she writes, is not "immunity from consequences," but not being hindered by "interpersonal fear"—the feeling of being rejected, blamed, or humiliated when you are speaking up or taking a risk.[8]

If people feel safe, they won't hold back with critical comments that can move an organization forward. If it is fine to openly speak about mistakes (especially your own), the whole team can learn and grow.

How do you create a fear-free environment?

In a fear-free environment, you will still have to bear the consequences of your actions (e.g. losing your job if you are really incompetent in a particular domain), but you will always be **treated fairly and respectfully in interpersonal encounters**. In such an environment, it will be safe for all team members to be candid and open, and they can be sure that others will not react badly to them if they make a mistake.

Building on Amy Edmondson's work, here are a few tips about what you as a leader can do to create a fear-free environment:[9]

- **Reframe failure.** That means first asking which type of failure you're dealing with: an avoidable one (because someone was just negligent), a complex one (caused by a 'systems failure,' a combination of several different factors), or an intelligent one (because someone tried something out that you can learn something from). The trick is not to ignore the failures, but to understand which category they are in, and to always ask the question *"What can we learn from it?"* rather than *"Who is to blame?"*
- **Emphasize the purpose.** Explain why and for whom it is important that the team performs well, and how an open and candid form of communication can help to make this possible.
- **Signal that it is OK for your team members to speak out.** You can do so, for example, by demonstrating 'situational humility' (admitting that you don't know the answer to everything), asking a lot of good questions, practicing active listening (see *Skill 14 Practice*

active listening), and creating 'official' spaces ('forums') in which you ask people to contribute.

- **Express your appreciation when people speak up and contribute** (listen and say thank you).
- **Destigmatize failure** through taking a solution- and learning-oriented approach, offering help, and looking forward.
- **Sanction clear violations.** Providing psychological safety doesn't mean that every behavior is acceptable. Leaders need to make boundaries clear, and there should also be consequences for people who repeatedly violate rules, show neglect for the psychological safety of others, or put other team members or the organization as a whole at risk.

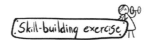

Creating a fear-free environment

Next time you or someone else in your team makes a mistake, take the following two steps:

1. **Identify the type of failure.** Was it an avoidable, complex, or intelligent failure?
2. **Ask what you can learn from the failure.** Discuss together with a team member (including if it was your own mistake) how you could use the mistake as an opportunity to learn how to ensure a better outcome for your team and the organization in future.

My personal notes about creating a fear-free environment

43 Provide challenges

What does providing challenges mean?

We all grow through **challenges**: complex and demanding tasks that we haven't done before.

When we are faced with a challenge, at first we often don't know how to proceed. We might even feel uncomfortable about it. But it's exactly because we need to **step out of our comfort zone**—and because we are forced to learn new skills to get the task accomplished—that challenges are the perfect development opportunities both for yourself as a leader as well as for your team members.

Why is providing challenges an important leadership skill?

There are a range of positive effects of providing challenges for your team members:

- **Challenges can make your team members smarter,** as they are acquiring new knowledge and skills along the way.

- **Challenges can make them stronger**, as they get a chance to build their problem-solving muscles, learn how to become more resilient, and enhance their self-efficacy (their belief in their own abilities) and self-esteem.
- **Challenges can be highly motivating.** Goal-setting theory—one of the most widely recognized modern motivational theories—suggests that challenging goals have a strong motivational effect, especially when they are accepted by a person and combined with feedback along the way (see *Skill 18 Harness the power of feedback*).[10]
- **Challenges can strengthen trust.** When you show your team members that you think they're capable of mastering a difficult challenge, and when they get the feeling that you believe in them, this will increase the level of trust in your relationship with them.

How do you provide challenges?

As a leader, you should ideally develop an eye for spotting development opportunities for your team members. Try out one or a combination of the following approaches:

- **Look for potential** in your team members rather than just seeing their current limitations. In which areas could they still develop their knowledge and skills to a higher level, and what kind of challenges could help them reach their potential?
- Whenever you have a new task to accomplish or delegate, ask yourself **for whom this might be a development opportunity**. Assign the task to that person rather than to someone who is already performing well in this particular domain.
- Ask your team members about **their personal development goals**, and think about which challenges could help them reach their goals.

Don't forget to include your team members in the process of defining the right challenges for them. Imposed challenges can actually be highly demotivating, especially if your team members already feel overloaded with work. Make sure to get their commitment to a challenge first, and offer additional support (e.g. in the form of training or coaching) if necessary.

Providing challenges for your team members

Here's one way you can provide challenges that are beneficial for your team members as well as for the organization:[11]

1. Think about the **future challenges that your organization and your team as a whole are facing.** Which skills will you need (as a team) to successfully master these challenges?
2. Assess the **current skills** in your team and compare them to the skills that you will need to succeed in the future.
3. Identify the **skills gap**: where do you need to develop new skills as a team?
4. Think about which **challenges you could provide** either for individual team members or the team as a whole in order to close the skills gap.

My personal notes about providing challenges

_____

_____

_____

_____

_____

_____

_____

_____

44 Coach your team members

What does coaching your team members mean?

In a leadership context, **coaching** is a purposeful interaction in which you as a leader use a smart questioning approach to help a team member think through challenging issues, raise their self-awareness, consider their options, and take the right actions to realize their full potential or achieve their work-related goals.[12]

Why is coaching your team members an important leadership skill?

Researchers have observed that coaching can have a range of positive outcomes for those who are being coached:[13]

- A **clearer focus** on what they want to achieve and how to achieve it.
- A higher level of **motivation** to work toward their goals.
- A higher degree of **self-awareness** (e.g. becoming more aware of their own goals, strengths, and development needs).

- Improved **self-confidence**, as the coaching process can lead to a better understanding of how to deal with certain issues.
- A positive impact on **work-related attitudes**.
- Enhanced **work performance**.
- Improved **problem-solving skills**.

In addition, there's a positive impact from the **feeling of being listened to,** and from getting the chance to see things in perspective.

The team and organization, in turn, will profit from higher productivity and improved work performance from team members who are being coached, as well as from their improved social and teamwork skills (if team-related issues are discussed in the coaching conversation).

How do you coach your team members?

As a leader, you can coach by **conducting goal-oriented coaching conversations** with your team members. In a coaching conversation, you take a structured approach in which you ask questions that help the team member better understand a problem situation, the goal they want to achieve, and the right way to hit that goal. Your job as a coach is not to provide answers, but to ask the right questions and then engage in active listening (see *Skill 14 Practice active listening*).

A widely used method for structuring a coaching conversation is the **GROW model**, in which you are asking questions that help your team member clarify the following points (in this order):[14]

- Goal: what do they want to achieve?
- Reality: what does the current situation look like?
- Options: what are the alternative courses of action for improving the situation?
- Will: what will they actually do to improve the situation? Which concrete action steps will they take?

As a leader, you can use this structure to help your team member clearly formulate their goals and explore what they could do to achieve them. You can then also act as an **accountability partner**, asking them at a later (ideally agreed) point in time whether they have implemented what they wanted to do, and what they have learned from it (or, alternatively, what they have learned from not being able to implement it).

Coaching your team members

Try to turn one of your next conversations with a team member (or with a friend) into a coaching conversation. Follow the four phases of the GROW model and ask goal-oriented questions such as:[15]

- **Goal:** *"What would you like to accomplish regarding this issue?", "What makes this goal important for you?", "How could you reformulate the goal so that it depends on your actions more than on external circumstances?", "How will you know that you have achieved your goal?"*
- **Reality:** *"What are the main factors that contributed to this situation?", "Who else is involved in the issue? What is their role? What are their interests?", "What are the main obstacles?", "What holds you back from taking action?"*
- **Options:** *"What could be a potential solution for the problem?", "What else could you do?", "What could you do to remove this obstacle?", "What would you need to do in order to make it happen?"*
- **Will:** *"What will you do?", "Which option will you pursue to achieve your goal?", "Which concrete action steps will you take?", "When will you put this into practice?"*

My personal notes about coaching my team members

---

45 Create learning and development opportunities

What does creating learning and development opportunities mean?

In addition to formal training seminars, coaching, or providing new challenges, there are also **alternative ways of providing opportunities for your team members to improve their knowledge and competencies.** Creating learning and development opportunities means actively designing and implementing learning processes that contribute to enhancing the skills of your team members.

Why is creating learning and development opportunities an important leadership skill?

It is one of your most important jobs as a leader to help your team members grow. Developing new skills or enhancing existing ones will not only make your team members more competent, they will also become more confident. New knowledge and skills will enable them to work more productively, take on new challenges, and better handle unexpected situations, which can be of great benefit for both your team members and the organization as a whole. Opportunities to learn something new can also (re-)energize your team and create and maintain a high level of engagement.

How do you create learning and development opportunities?

There are several ways of creating learning and development opportunities for your team members:[16]

1. **Create shadowing opportunities.** That's when you let one team member accompany and observe another one (or you as a leader) for a certain period of time, for example a day or week. This can help to broaden the skills base of the team member, and at the same time creates opportunities for promoting cross-functional or cross-departmental collaboration.

2. **Encourage and organize cross-training between team members.** Everyone in your team undoubtedly has some special skills. Why don't you ask your numbers guy to train the other team members in some basic data analytics methods? Or ask the tech wizard in the team to report on the newest developments in the field. Cross-training between team members can also help team members appreciate the strengths of their colleagues, and can boost the self-confidence of those who get a chance to share their knowledge and skills.

3. **Use the power of mentoring.** Ask a more experienced team member to become a mentor for a junior member. Mentors can provide guidance and support, act as a sounding board, and help build a network. (As a leader, you can also be mentored by team members who are more experienced in one particular domain, e.g. by a young tech wizard in technology-related issues.)

4. **Organize a team book club**, where you and your team members read professional books that are relevant for your team's work. Then discuss the learnings and implications for your team together with them.

5. **Provide additional responsibilities outside the job description.**
Offering chances to learn new things from assignments outside of team members' formal roles can broaden their skills base, and maybe also open new career possibilities for them.

To ensure such learning arrangements have a positive motivational effect, do not impose them on team members. Real engagement develops when people are fully involved, not only in the learning process but also in choosing what and how to learn.

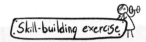

Creating learning and development opportunities

Write down the name of one of your team members on a blank sheet of paper. Then note down the skills that you think this person could or should develop in order to become more effective in their job or to prepare for the next step in their career. Think about how you could use one or several of the five types of learning and development opportunities above to develop or enhance these skills. Try to be concrete, e.g. thinking about which person could be assigned as a 'shadowing target' or a mentor.

My personal notes about creating learning and development opportunities

_____
_____
_____
_____
_____
_____
_____

46 Engage your team members

What does it mean to engage your team members?

Team members are **engaged** when they are dedicated to giving their best and performing well in their jobs, with a deep commitment to the success of both their team and the organization. For engaged team members, their work is more than just 'a job.' They are passionate about what they do, and have a strong **positive emotional connection** with their work.

Of course, engagement cannot be imposed, but your actions as a leader can have a strong impact on the level of engagement in your team.

Why is engaging your team members an important leadership skill?

A high level of engagement in your team can have a range of different benefits:[17]

- Studies have shown **a strong link between engagement and performance outcomes.**
- There's also a positive association between engagement and the **well-being and life satisfaction of employees.**

- Employees with high levels of engagement tend to have a **lower intention to quit their jobs** (which lowers turnover rates).
- Engaged team members can have a positive **motivational effect on others in your team.**

Last but not least, engaged team members are typically **more open to learning and developing themselves**, which in turn contributes to the development of your whole team.

How do you engage your team members?

Leadership expert Steve Radcliffe identifies **four key aspects of engagement:**[18]

1. Make sure that **people feel valued in their relationships with you as a leader.** You can do so by giving them the feeling that they are listened to, that you care about their opinion, and that you want them to be involved (see *Skill 14 Practice active listening*). It's about consciously building a relationship in addition to just 'getting the work done.'
2. Invite team members to **co-invent the future.** Actively include them in thinking about what the future could look like for your organization and which steps need to be taken to get there (instead of just telling them what you would like to do).
3. Focus on **specific opportunities and priorities** together with your team members. Put your heads together and discuss how you could excel in a particular area that you, as a team, would like to focus your efforts on (see *Skill 24 Set the right priorities*).
4. Be very **clear about what you expect**: Results are achieved when people take action, so once you have agreed on your team's priorities for the future, it's also time to clearly articulate your expectations.

It makes a big difference if you try to actively engage team members rather than just telling them what to do—if they get the feeling that they are active co-creators of their future, not just passively taking orders. As Radcliffe says, as a leader, you can see every interaction as an opportunity to engage your team members.[19]

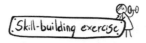

Engaging your team members

Next time you are about to start a new initiative, try to deliberately think about how you could use this as an opportunity for engaging your team members.

Try to refrain from 'communicating' or telling them what you intend to do. Involve them in co-inventing the future and set priorities together instead. Give them the feeling that you really care about their opinion.

When you've had a good discussion about what you would like to do together, don't forget to be very clear on what you're expecting from your team members.

My personal notes about engaging my team members

47 Address performance problems

What does addressing performance problems mean?

People are not machines. We all have our better and worse days. Sometimes we are more motivated, sometimes less. And we are not always capable of performing at the same high level. We all 'underperform' compared to our usual standards on some days. An empathetic leader knows and accepts this, and will not be too harsh on team members who are just having one of their worse days.

When team members continually show **poor performance** (meaning that they are not able to meet the basic requirements of their job), however, it is your job as a leader to explicitly address it, identify the **underlying reasons** for the performance problem, and then **discuss and solve the problem** together with the team member.

Why is addressing performance problems an important leadership skill?

It is obvious that continual poor performance can lead to negative outcomes for your organization. If team members are unable to complete their work to a reasonable standard of quality and/or in the agreed timeframe, it can have a negative impact on customers or other people who are dependent on that work being properly done.

In addition, one team member who constantly underperforms can trigger a domino effect and poison the morale of the whole team. As a leader, you are responsible for the performance of the whole team. That's why you need to address performance problems when they arise.

How do you address performance problems?

To address performance problems, you have to work a bit like a doctor who is trying to cure an illness:

1. Recognize the symptoms
2. Diagnose the root cause
3. Find the right therapy

Symptoms for performance problems could be a lot of missed deadlines, absenteeism, poor engagement levels, or repeated complaints from other team members or customers.

When you notice such symptoms, it's time to dig a bit deeper and try to find out what's wrong. You will only be able to **diagnose the right root cause** in a dialogue with the team member. It is important to do so without delay, even if you feel uncomfortable about it. Give timely feedback to the person about your perceptions (see *Skill 18 Harness the power of feedback*), apply what you have learned about mastering tough conversations (see *Skill 19 Master tough conversations*), and try to uncover—ideally with a questioning approach rather than with a preconceived opinion—the root cause for the performance problem.

Potential root causes are:[20]

- Non-work-related challenges like health problems or personal issues
- Tiredness and fatigue
- A lack of resources
- A lack of competences or skills
- The feeling of being unfairly treated (maybe regarding their salary) or not getting enough support
- No room for development and growth
- Work overload and work-related stress

- Motivational issues (e.g. not finding meaning in the work, not having enough challenges, or being bored)
- Unclear expectations
- Interpersonal issues in the workplace (e.g. conflicts with colleagues)
- Demotivating leadership behavior

As the last few points show, the root cause doesn't necessarily have to lie with the team member themselves—others (including you as a leader) can also be the source of the problem (or at least be involved in it).

Once you've identified a concrete root cause in an open discussion with your team member, try to find the right **therapy**. That could be, for example, providing resources, providing training or new challenges, or addressing conflicts within the team. The important point here is to **match the therapy with the root cause**.

If the intervention does not work, enter into another dialogue with your team member, make your expectations clear, and try again. If nothing works, it's maybe time to think about reassigning the person to another job which is more suitable for them.

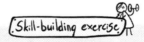

Determining the reasons for high and low performance

Use this exercise to better understand the reasons for fluctuations in performance:

1. Observe your own performance for a certain period of time (e.g. 2–3 weeks). At the end of each day, assess your performance level on that day on a scale of 1 = 'very low' to 10 = 'world-class.' Note down a few keywords in which you describe what you think are the reasons for the high or low performance.
2. If you would like to coach a team member, ask them to conduct the same exercise. Then discuss the results with them following a coaching approach (see *Skill 44 Coach your team members*).

48 Manage change

What does it mean to manage change?

Leading always means leading *somewhere*: taking a team from where they are today toward achieving a certain goal in the future. To get from A to B, some things will have to change. **Managing change** means taking a structured approach to initiating and implementing a transition or trans- formation process in your organization. It is important to **involve your team members in the process** so that they will support or at least not unnecessarily impede the change.

Why is managing change an important leadership skill?

Growth and development—whether on a personal or organizational level—is not possible without change. If you would like to help others or your organization grow and develop, therefore, you need to understand how to manage change. "In reality all leadership is about change," says best-selling leadership author Chris Hirst. "By definition, leadership can- not be about the maintenance of the status quo."[21]

Deliberately managing change is also important because it can be quite challenging for people to change. Maybe you have seen the cartoon in which someone asks *"Who wants change?"* and everyone is raising their hands. When the question changes to *"Who wants to change?"* everyone is just looking down at the ground. People often fear that change is disadvantageous for them, and that's why it's important to consider and address the interests and feelings of the people who are affected by a change.[22]

How do you effectively manage change?

Here are a few points to consider for your next change initiative:[23]

1. **Have a good reason for the change.** People will only be willing to change when they understand why it is necessary. Change management expert John Kotter therefore sees "creating a sense of urgency" as the first task of a leader in managing change.

2. **Involve key people first.** Before you publicly announce a change, try to get the support of key people in your team as well as influential stakeholders. Officially start a change initiative only after you have secured their commitment in personal one-to-one talks.

3. **Involve your team in the change process.** Instead of just telling them what to do differently, try to get ideas from team members about how to implement the change. People who are given a voice in a change process are much more likely to accept the change.

4. **Communicate very clearly.** Uncertainty is one of the biggest sources of fear during a change situation. Be sure to clearly and simply communicate, therefore, what will change, why it will change, what is the goal to be achieved, how the change will be implemented, and—very importantly—how the change will affect your team members.

5. **Frame the change as an experiment.** When people are unsure whether a particular change is a good idea, it's sometimes easier to agree on trying something out together to see how it will work, while keeping the possibility open of reversing the decision if things don't work out as planned.

6. **Ensure 'quick wins.'** It can have a strong motivational effect on your team if they see that some of your change initiatives are quickly implemented and that they actually change things for the better.

7. **Review progress.** Regularly check if you are staying on track (e.g. with the use of key performance indicators), and keep talking about

the change with your team (positive reinforcement for people who are contributing a lot to the change effort is particularly important here).

8. **Celebrate success.** Don't forget to pause and say thank you to your team for achieving the change goals.

Don't expect things to remain smooth and easy during a period of change. Expect problems along the way and allow some time for acceptance,[24] but at the same time continue to spread positive energy (see *Skill 03 Spread positive energy*).

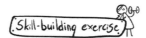

Prepare for effectively managing change

Before starting your next change initiative, try to answer the following questions first:

- What are the compelling reasons for the change, and what are the potential benefits?
- Who are the key people that need to be involved before you officially start the change initiative?
- Who could be negatively affected by the change, and how will you communicate with them to avoid or mitigate resistance?
- Which 'quick wins' could be fast and easy to implement?

My personal notes about managing change

49 Organize reflective sessions

What does it mean to organize reflective sessions?

A **reflective session** is time that is specifically set aside for you and your team to "reflect upon what you do, how you do it, and why you do it."[25] It takes you out of your day-to-day work and allows you to deliberately change from a 'doing' mode into a 'learning' mode.

Why is organizing reflective sessions an important leadership skill?

The effectiveness of reflective sessions as a tool to improve the performance of a team has been noted in different contexts. Examples include **quality circles** that have helped to skyrocket quality levels in Japanese firms, **sprint retrospective meetings** in agile work teams (meetings that are held at the end of short, intense work periods to discuss what went well and what could be improved next time—see *Skill 37 Create an agile team*), or regular (e.g. annual) **strategy cycles** that allow the management of an organization to recalibrate the overall goals and direction.

Holding reflective sessions with your team from time to time can reap the following benefits:

- It's a **great learning opportunity** which allows your team to grow, improves collaboration, and enhances performance and productivity.
- It's an **opportunity to celebrate achievements** together with your team, which feels good and can also contribute to bonding within the team.
- It can help to **create a fear-free environment**, as you're providing a 'safe space' in which you deliberately invite your team to speak up and raise critical comments (see *Skill 42 Create a fear-free environment*).
- It's an **opportunity to engage team members**, as you are taking your time to ask for their opinions and listen to their ideas (see *Skill 46 Engage your team members*).
- It can help you **avoid making the same mistakes twice**, and help you anticipate future problems before they occur.

How do you organize a reflective session?

Reflective sessions are relatively straightforward to organize. Just call your team together after having finished a project, when you have completed an important milestone in a project, or at another point in time when you have the feeling that your team could profit from taking a short time out to reflect upon why and how you are working together.

Tell everyone about the purpose of the meeting (to learn from each other how you could improve your joint work) and ask them to prepare answers to the following four questions:

1. **What went well** in our joint work (e.g. in project X) and what would we like to keep doing in the future?
2. **What didn't go so well** and what would we therefore prefer to stop doing?
3. **What could we improve** (or do differently) next time?
4. **Where should we set our focus** for the next steps?

Go through those four questions in the team meeting and make sure to ask everyone in the team to candidly voice their opinions. At the end of the meeting, agree on a short action plan (preferably with just a few action steps that you're really committing to), which you then distribute to all team members in written form.

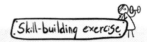

Organizing a Start-Stop-Continue retrospective

A slightly different way of framing the questions from above is the **Start-Stop-Continue** technique for agile retrospectives (which you can also use as a guideline for your next reflective session).

After completing a team task, get together with your team and try to answer the following three questions:[25]

1. **Start**—what should we as a team start doing in future?
2. **Stop**—what should we stop doing?
3. **Continue**—what should we continue doing?

Use a visual aid (either a flipchart, whiteboard or virtual board) to note down the feedback from the team.

My personal notes about organizing reflective sessions

_____

_____

_____

_____

_____

_____

_____

_____

50 Be a role model in developing yourself

What does being a role model in developing yourself mean?

If you are accepted by your team members as a leader, your attitudes and actions can have a strong impact on them. Research results confirm that a transition to a new leader can also lead to a change of attitudes among team members.[27] You can use this 'role model effect' to **emphasize the importance of personal growth**.

When you exhibit a learner's mindset, show that you are open to learning new ideas, and personally engage in learning activities, you are setting an example for others in your team. Chances are high that it will encourage them to grow and develop too.

Why is being a role model in developing yourself an important leadership skill?

"Growth is the great separator between those who succeed and those who don't,"[28] writes leadership expert John C. Maxwell. This is true for your own personal growth as a leader as well as for the development of your team as a whole. A focus on personal development not only strengthens your knowledge and skills base, it can also help you expand your perspective, grow your confidence, and make both you and your team more successful.

By being a role model in developing yourself, you as a leader can contribute to creating a **learning culture** in your team. You can develop a community in which everyone continually seeks to acquire new knowledge and skills to improve both their personal and the organization's performance.

How do you become a role model in developing yourself?

Here's what you can do as a leader to become a role model in self-development for your team members:

- **Exhibit a learner's mindset.** Instead of adopting a 'know-it-all' attitude, you can show your openness and willingness to learn, for example through being curious about how things work, admitting that you don't know things, inviting others to explain something to you, and asking questions instead of having all the answers. With the right mindset, every encounter with other people can become an opportunity for you to learn and grow.
- **Be willing to leave your comfort zone.** Your learning curve will be particularly steep when you are faced with challenging tasks (see *Skill 43 Provide challenges*). Try to challenge yourself with new tasks from time to time (for example, working a week on the shop floor if you are a senior manager), with the clear goal of learning new skills and broadening your perspective.
- **Take part in learning activities.** Don't just organize training seminars for your team members, but actively take part in them too.
- **Discuss your learnings with your team members.** Use reflective sessions to ask others what they have learned (see *Skill 49 Organize reflective sessions*), but don't forget to tell them what you have learned too—especially from mistakes that you have made.
- **Frequently ask the question "What can we learn from that?"** The words you choose contribute to creating reality. Speaking about learning will help you and your team to never stop learning.

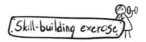

Your next personal development steps

Use the following six questions to identify the next steps in your personal development:

1. Which 'big thing' would you like to accomplish or achieve in the future?
2. What's your motivation—why would you like to achieve that?
3. Which knowledge and skills will you need to develop to accomplish your goal in a way that will make you really proud of yourself?
4. In order to prioritize—what is the one knowledge or skills area that, if developed to a higher level, will make the biggest difference for achieving your goal?
5. Which concrete development steps will you take (and by when) to compel yourself to a higher level in this knowledge or skills area?
6. How can you ensure that others in your team will be able to profit from your knowledge and skills development initiative too?

My personal notes about becoming a role model in developing myself

_____

_____

_____

_____

_____

_____

_____

_____

A concluding note

Let's face it: leadership cannot be learned in a day (not even with a book like this one). Good leaders always see themselves as being on **a lifelong development journey**. I hope that you have found this book inspiring and useful for accompanying you part of the way along your own personal leadership development journey.

If you've read all the chapters, and if you have also completed some of the skill-building exercises, you should already have begun to recognize some changes in the way you lead.

I hope that you've

- gained **more confidence** in your leadership role,
- received **positive feedback** on the way you communicate,
- been able to **set the right priorities** for both yourself and your team,
- contributed to **creating a well-functioning team**, and
- **supported others** on their own personal growth path.

This not only makes you a better leader, but also a person who is really making a difference, both for the organization you work or volunteer for and in the lives of others.

If you think that this book—or maybe just a few of the ideas within it—has made a difference in your own learning journey and could also be of benefit to your team members, colleagues, students, or friends, please share it with them!

As an independent author and publisher with a mission to create concise, approachable and affordable books that can make a difference to a wider audience, I would be particularly grateful if you could help to spread the word about this book through writing an honest online review.

It takes just one or two minutes to write a few lines, but it could have a big positive impact. The more people improve their leadership skills, the more of society's problems will we be able to solve in a culture of collaboration, teamwork and trust.

If you're interested in staying informed about current developments in the field and getting more information about new books for smart learners, you are also welcome to visit *www.econcise.com/newsletter* and subscribe to our newsletter.

Last but not least, let me just say **thank you** for taking this book into your hands and for being part of the community of excellent leaders who understand that leading others well always starts with leading and developing yourself first. Together with Eva, the creator of the 'little superhero' that accompanied you through this book in her drawings, we wish you all the best for continuing your journey of becoming a better leader, day by day!

Endnotes

Chapter 1 Develop a leadership mindset

[1] Lubar, K., & Halpern, B. L. (2004). *Leadership Presence: Dramatic Techniques to Reach Out, Motivate, and Inspire.* New York, NY: Avery, p. 3.

[2] Fox Cabane, O. (2012). *The Charisma Myth: Master the Art of Personal Magnetism.* London: Portfolio Penguin, p. 4.

[3] Ibid, p. 6.

[4] Lubar, K., & Halpern, B. L. (2004). *Leadership Presence: Dramatic Techniques to Reach Out, Motivate, and Inspire.* New York, NY: Avery.

[5] Strycharczyk, D., Clough, P., & Perry, J. (2021). *Developing Mental Toughness: Strategies to Improve Performance, Resilience and Wellbeing in Individuals and Organizations.* 3rd ed. London: Kogan Page, pp. 101–105.

[6] Ibid, p. 104.

[7] Ibid, p. 108.

[8] Fox Cabane, O. (2012). *The Charisma Myth: Master the Art of Personal Magnetism.* London: Portfolio Penguin, p. 141.

[9] The research study that originally claimed evidence for a strong "fake it 'til you make it" effect is Carney, D. R., Cuddy, A. J., & Yap, A. J. (2010). Power posing: Brief nonverbal displays affect neuroendocrine levels and risk tolerance. *Psychological Science, 21*(10), 1363–1368. The research has raised a lot of controversy, however. Two key contributions to this discussion are Simmons, J. P., & Simonsohn, U. (2017). Power posing: P-curving the evidence. *Psychological Science, 28*(5), 687–693 and Cuddy, A. J., Schultz, S. J., & Fosse, N. E. (2018). P-curving a more comprehensive body of research on postural feedback reveals clear evidential value for power-posing effects: Reply to Simmons and Simonsohn (2017). *Psychological Science, 29*(4), 656–666.

[10] Based on Fox Cabane, O. (2012). *The Charisma Myth: Master the Art of Personal Magnetism.* London: Portfolio Penguin, p. 241.

[11] Malinga, K. S., Stander, M., & Nell, W. (2019). Positive leadership: Moving towards an integrated definition and interventions. In: L. E. Van Zyl and S. Rothman Sr. (eds.), *Theoretical Approaches to Multi-Cultural Positive Psychological Interventions* (pp. 201–228). Cham: Springer Nature Switzerland.

[12] Clarkson, B. G., Wagstaff, C. R., Arthur, C. A., & Thelwell, R. C. (2020). Leadership and the contagion of affective phenomena: A systematic review and mini meta-analysis. *European Journal of Social Psychology, 50*(1), 61–80, p. 61.

[13] Robbins, A. (2001). *Awaken the Giant Within: Take Immediate Control of Your Mental, Emotional, Physical and Financial Destiny.* London: Simon & Schuster UK/Pocket Books, pp. 216–222.

[14] Kraft, T. L., & Pressman, S. D. (2012). Grin and bear it: The influence of manipulated facial expression on the stress response. *Psychological Science, 23*(11), 1372–1378.

[15] Younger, H. R. (2021). *The Art of Caring Leadership: How Leading With Heart Uplifts Teams and Organizations.* San Francisco, CA: Berrett-Koehler Publishers, p. 1.

[16] Chan, S. C., & Mak, W. M. (2012). Benevolent leadership and follower performance: The mediating role of leader–member exchange (LMX). *Asia Pacific Journal of Management, 29*(2), 285–301.

[17] Houston, M. (2021). The art of caring leadership in business can increase ROI. Forbes. https://www.forbes.com/sites/melissahouston/2021/06/16/the-art-of-caring-leadership-in-business-can-increase-roi/?sh=46f7e2422dad. Published 16 June 2021, accessed 23 March 2022.

[18] Younger, H. R. (2021). *The Art of Caring Leadership: How Leading With Heart Uplifts Teams and Organizations.* San Francisco, CA: Berrett-Koehler Publishers.

[19] Ibid.

[20] The idea of growth mindset versus fixed mindset was introduced by Stanford psychology professor Carol Dweck. Her most popular book is Dweck, C. (2006). *Mindset: The New Psychology of Success.* New York, NY: Ballantine Books.

[21] Kouzes, T. K., & Posner, B. Z. (2019). Influence of managers' mindset on leadership behavior. *Leadership & Organization Development Journal, 40*(8), pp. 829–844, p. 829.

[22] Strycharczyk, D., Clough, P., & Perry, J. (2021). *Developing Mental Toughness: Strategies to Improve Performance, Resilience and Wellbeing in Individuals and Organizations.* 3rd ed. London: Kogan Page, pp. 53; 57.

[23] Peters, S. (2012). *The Chimp Paradox: The Mind Management Programme for Confidence, Success and Happiness.* London: Vermilion.

[24] A similar exercise was proposed by Peters, S. (2012). *The Chimp Paradox: The Mind Management Programme for Confidence, Success and Happiness.* London: Vermilion, pp. 211–212.

[25] Sternad, D. (2020). *Effective Management: Developing Yourself, Others and Organizations.* London: Red Globe Press.

[26] Mind Tools (n.d.). What are your values? https://www.mindtools.com/pages/article/newTED_85.htm. Accessed 25 March 2022.

[27] This exercise is taken from Sternad, D. (2020), *Effective Management: Developing Yourself, Others and Organizations*, Red Globe Press, p. 66. Reproduced with permission of Bloomsbury Publishing plc.

[28] Strycharczyk, D., Clough, P., & Perry, J. (2021). *Developing Mental Toughness: Strategies to Improve Performance, Resilience and Wellbeing in Individuals and Organizations.* 3rd ed. London: Kogan Page, p. 71.

[29] Li, J., Zhang, J., & Yang, Z. (2017). Associations between a leader's work passion and an employee's work passion: a moderated mediation model. *Frontiers in Psychology, 8,* https://www.frontiersin.org/article/10.3389/fpsyg.2017.01447.

[30] Clear, J. (2018). *Atomic Habits: An Easy and Proven Way to Build Good Habits and Break Bad Ones.* London: Random House Business Books.

[31] Maxwell, J. C. (2013). *Sometimes You Win, Sometimes You Learn: Life's Greatest Lessons Are Gained From Our Losses.* New York, NY: Center Street.

[32] Bailey, J. R., & Rehman, S. (2022). Don't underestimate the power of self-reflection. https://hbr.org/2022/03/dont-underestimate-the-power-of-self-reflection, published 4 March 2022, accessed 11 July 2022.

[33] Ibid.

[34] Ibid.

[35] Lanaj, K., Foulk, T. A., & Erez, A. (2019). Energizing leaders via self-reflection: A within-person field experiment. *Journal of Applied Psychology, 104*(1), 1–18.

[36] This exercise is based on three questions proposed by Driscoll, J. (1994). Reflective practice for practise. *Senior Nurse, 14*(1), 47–50.

Chapter 2 Communicate with impact

[1] Watzlawick, P., Bavelas, J. B., & Jackson, D. D. (1967). *Pragmatics of Human Communication: A Study of Interactional Patterns, Pathologies and Paradoxes.* New York, NY: W. W. Norton.

[2] Marquet, D. L. (2020). *Leadership is Language: The Hidden Power of What You Say—and What You Don't.* London: Penguin Random House, pp. 130–31.

[3] Robbins, A. (2001). *Awaken the Giant Within: Take Immediate Control of Your Mental, Emotional, Physical and Financial Destiny.* London: Simon & Schuster/Pocket Books, pp. 179–180.

[4] Ibid, p. 182.

[5] Ibid, p. 193.

[6] Navarro, J., & Sciarra Pointer, T. (2021). *Be Exceptional: Master the Five Traits that Set Extraordinary People Apart.* London: Thorsons.

[7] Ibid.

[8] Barker, A. (2019). *Improve Your Communication Skills: How to Build Trust, Be Heard and Communicate With Confidence.* 5th ed. London: Kogan Page, p. 72.

[12] Brown, B. (2020). *Interview with Brené Brown on courage, vulnerability, + never listening to the critics.* https://www.mantramagazine.com/single-post/2020/04/24/interview-with-bren%C3%A9-brown-on-courage-vulnerability-and-never-listening-to-the-critics, published 24 April 2020, accessed 16 Feburary 2022.

[13] Folkman, J. R. (2006). *The Power of Feedback: 35 Principles for Turning Feedback from Others Into Personal and Professional Change.* Hoboken, NY: John Wiley & Sons, p. xv.

[14] Dweck, C. S. (2006). *Mindset: The New Psychology of Success.* New York, NY: Random House.

[15] Barker, A. (2019). *Improve Your Communication Skills: How to Build Trust, Be Heard and Communicate With Confidence.* 5th ed. London: Kogan Page, p. 62.

[16] Patterson, K., Grenny, J., McMillan, R., & Switzler, A. (2012). *Crucial Conversations: Tools for Talking When the Stakes Are High.* 2nd ed. New York, NY: McGraw-Hill, p. 3.

[17] Patterson, K., Grenny, J., McMillan, R., & Switzler, A. (2012). *Crucial Conversations: Tools for Talking When the Stakes Are High.* 2nd ed. New York, NY: McGraw-Hill.

[18] Ibid, p. 133.

Chapter 3 Clarify purpose and priorities

[1] Grant, A. M. (2012). Leading with meaning: Beneficiary contact, prosocial impact, and the performance effects of transformational leadership. *Academy of Management Journal, 55*(2), 458–476.

[2] Katzenbach, J. R., & Smith, D. K. (1993). The discipline of teams. *Harvard Business Review,* March/April. 111–120, p. 113.

[3] PeopleLeaders (n.d.). How to create a team purpose statement in three steps (and why). *https://peopleleaders.com.au/create-team-purpose-statement-in-three-steps/,* accessed 16 December 2022.

[4] Sternad, D. (2020). *Effective Management: Developing Yourself, Others and Organizations.* London: Red Globe Press, p. 216.

[5] Lafley, A. G., & Martin, R. L. (2013). *Playing to Win: How Strategy Really Works.* Boston, MA: Harvard Business Review Press.

[6] Extended from the 'From-To' framework presented by Sola, D., & Couturier, J. (2014). *How to Think Strategically: Your Roadmap to Innovation and Results.* Harlow: Pearson Education Limited, pp. 151; 216.

[7] merriam-webster.com (n.d.). Goal. *https://www.merriam-webster.com/dictionary/goal,* accessed 21 December 2022.

[8] Minto, B. (2008). *The Pyramid Principle.* 3rd ed. Harlow: Financial Times Prentice Hall; Pelard, F. (2020). *How to Be Strategic.* London: Penguin Business.

[9] Drucker, P. (1967). *The Effective Executive.* New York, NY: Harper & Row, p. 24.

[10] Sternad, D. (2020). *Effective Management: Developing Yourself, Others and Organizations.* London: Red Globe Press, p. 44.

[11] McKeon, G. (2020). *Essentialism: The Disciplined Pursuit of Less.* Trade paperback edition. New York, NY: Currency, p. 23.

[12] Sternad, D. (2021). *Solve It! The Mindset and Tools of Smart Problem Solvers.* Moosburg: econcise, p. 94.

[13] Sternad, D. (2020). *Effective Management: Developing Yourself, Others and Organizations.* London: Red Globe Press, p. 89.

[14] Ibid, p. 89.

[15] Ibid, p. 88.

[16] This exercise is based on ideas presented in Canfield, J., & Switzer, J. (2004). Complete delegation exercise. http://www.thesuccessprinciples.com/resource/TSP-DelegationExercise.pdf, accessed 23 December 2022.

[17] Sternad, D. (2021). *Solve It! The Mindset and Tools of Smart Problem Solvers.* Moosburg: econcise, p. 1.

[18] Pittino, D. (2022). *The Concise Leadership Textbook: Essential Knowledge and Skills for Developing Yourself as a Leader.* Moosburg: econcise, p. 15.

[19] Ibid, p. 17.

[20] Sternad, D. (2021). *Solve It! The Mindset and Tools of Smart Problem Solvers.* Moosburg: econcise.

[21] Ibid.

[22] Dholakia, U. M. (2017). What is a "good" decision. https://www.psychologytoday.com/us/blog/the-science-behind-behavior/201707/what-is-good-decision, published 9 July 2017, accessed 30 December 2022.

[23] kanbanize.com (n.d.). What is a bottleneck and how to deal with it? https://kanbanize.com/lean-management/pull/what-is-bottleneck, accessed 2 January 2023.

[24] Malik, F. (2015). *Managing Performing Living: Effective Management for a New World*. Frankfurt am Main: Campus, p. 330.

[25] Hyatt, M. (2019). *Free to Focus: A Total Productivity System to Achieve More By Doing Less*. Grand Rapids, MI: Baker Books, p. 108.

[25] Based on ideas in: Hyatt, M. (2019). *Free to Focus: A Total Productivity System to Achieve More By Doing Less*. Grand Rapids, MI: Baker Books, p. 110.

[26] Ibid.

[27] The following suggestions are based on Burkeman, O. (2021). *Four Thousand Weeks: Time and How to Use It*. London: The Bodley Head.

Chapter 4 Build a winning team

[1] Jordan, M. (1994). *I Can't Accept Not Trying: Michael Jordan on the Pursuit of Excellence*. San Francisco, CA: Harper San Francisco, pp. 20–24.

[2] Rath, T., & Conchie, B. (2000). *Strengths-Based Leadership: Great Leaders, Teams, and Why People Follow*. New York, NY: Gallup Press, p. 21.

[3] Bryant, A. (n.d.). How to hire the right person. https://www.nytimes.com/guides/business/how-to-hire-the-right-person, accessed 8 October 2022; Sternad, D. (2020). *Effective Management: Developing Yourself, Others and Organizations*. London: Red Globe Press.

[4] Some of these ideas are based on Bryant, A. (n.d.). How to hire the right person. https://www.nytimes.com/guides/business/how-to-hire-the-right-person, accessed 8 October 2022.

[5] These and other team roles were proposed by Belbin, R. M. (2012). *Team Roles at Work*. 2nd ed. London: Routledge.

[6] Some of these questions are based on Sternad, D. (2020). *Effective Management: Developing Yourself, Others and Organizations*. London: Red Globe Press, p. 118.

[7] Lee, P., Gillespie, N., Mann, L., & Wearing, A. (2010). Leadership and trust: Their effect on knowledge sharing and team performance. *Management Learning, 41*(4), 473–491.

[8] Citrin, J. M., & DeRosa, D. (2021). No trust, no team: Six best practices for building trust on virtual teams. https://www.spencerstuart.com/leadership-matters/2021/march/no-trust-no-team, published 25 March 2021, accessed 19 August 2022; Crowe Associated Ltd. (n.d.). The importance of trust in teams. http://www.crowe-associates.co.uk/teams-and-groups/the-importance-of-trust-in-teams/, accessed 19 August 2022.

[9] Timms, M. (2022). 5 ways leaders can build trust no matter where their teams work. https://www.fastcompany.com/90728111/5-ways-leaders-can-build-trust-no-matter-where-their-teams-work, published 10 March 2022, accessed 19 August 2022.

[10] Patterson, K., Grenny, J., Maxfield, D., McMillan, R., & Switzler, A. (2013). *Crucial Accountability: Tools for Resolving Violated Expectations, Broken Commitments, and Bad Behavior*. 2nd ed. New York, NY: McGraw Hill.

[11] Ibid.

[12] Sternad, D. (2020). *Effective Management: Developing Yourself, Others and Organizations*. London: Red Globe Press.

[13] Hanabury, E., & Stoddart, L. (2020). How to lead virtual teams successfully. https://www8.gsb.columbia.edu/articles/columbia-business/how-lead-virtual-teams-successfully, published 28 May 2020, accessed 17 August 2022; Pittino, D. (2022). *The Concise Leadership Textbook: Essential Knowledge and Skills for Developing Yourself as a Leader*. Moosburg: econcise; Sternad, D. (2020). *Effective Management: Developing Yourself, Others and Organizations*. London: Red Globe Press; Sternad, D. (2021). The challenges of managing remotely. https://youtu.be/PatLR8Pr-QA, video published 1 February 2021, accessed 17 August 2022.

[14] Clayton, S. J. (2021). An agile approach to change management. *Harvard Business Review*. https://hbr.org/2021/01/an-agile-approach-to-change-management, published 12 January 2021, accessed July 2022; Pittino, D. (2022). *The Concise Leadership Textbook: Essential Knowledge and Skills for Developing Yourself as a Leader*. Moosburg: econcise.

[15] scrum.org (n.d.). What is scrum? https://www.scrum.org/resources/what-is-scrum, accessed 17 August 2022.

[16] scrum.org (n.d.). What is sprint planning? https://www.scrum.org/resources/what-is-sprint-planning, accessed 17 August 2022.

[17] Pittino, D. (2022). *The Concise Leadership Textbook: Essential Knowledge and Skills for Developing Yourself as a Leader*. Moosburg: econcise; Sternad, D. (2020). *Effective Management: Developing Yourself, Others and Organizations*. London: Red Globe Press.

[18] Silva, T., Cunha, M. P. E., Clegg, S. R., Neves, P., Rego, A., & Rodrigues, R. A. (2014). Smells like team spirit: Opening a paradoxical black box. *Human Relations, 67*(3), 287–310.

[19] Carron, A. V., Bray, S. R., & Eys, M. A. (2002). Team cohesion and team success in sport. *Journal of Sports Sciences, 20*(2), 119–126; Mach, M., Dolan, S., & Tzafrir, S. (2010). The differential effect of team members' trust on team performance: The mediation role of team cohesion. *Journal of Occupational and Organizational Psychology, 83*(3), 771–794; Paul, R., Drake, J. R., & Liang, H. (2016). Global virtual team performance: The effect of coordination effectiveness, trust, and team cohesion. *IEEE Transactions on Professional Communication, 59*(3), 186–202.

[20] Pittino, D. (2022). *The Concise Leadership Textbook: Essential Knowledge and Skills for Developing Yourself as a Leader*. Moosburg: econcise; Townsend, J., Phillips, J. S., & Elkins, T. J. (2000). Employee retaliation: The neglected consequence of poor leader–member exchange relations. *Journal of Occupational Health Psychology, 5*(4), 457–463.

[21] Some of these suggestions are based on Carron, A.V., Eys, M.A., & Burke, S.M. (2007). Team cohesion. In: Jowett S., & Lavallee, D. (eds.), *Social Psychology in Sport* (pp. 91–102). Champaign, IL: Human Kinetics.

[22] Hill, L., & Lineback, K. (2011). *Being the Boss: The 3 Imperatives for Becoming a Great Leader*. Boston, MA: Harvard Business School Publishing; Sternad, D. (2020). *Effective Management: Developing Yourself, Others and Organizations*. London: Red Globe Press.

Chapter 5 Help others grow

[1] Kennedy, J. F. (1963). Remarks prepared for delivery at the Trade Mart in Dallas, TX, November 22, 1963 [undelivered]. https://www.jfklibrary.org/archives/other-resources/john-f-kennedy-speeches/dallas-tx-trade-mart-undelivered-19631122, accessed 26 January 2023. [John F. Kennedy planned to deliver the speech with this quote on the day of his death.]

[2] Gallup (2009). The strengths of leadership. https://news.gallup.com/businessjournal/113956/strengths-leadership.aspx, published 26 February 2009, accessed 9 August 2022.

[3] Ibid.

[4] CliftonStrengths (n.d.). What is a strength? https://www.strengthsquest.com/help/general/142466/strength.aspx, accessed 8 August 2022.

[5] This exercise is based on Sternad, D. (2020). *Effective Management: Developing Yourself, Others and Organizations*. London: Red Globe Press, p. 64.

[6] Rozovsky, J. (2015). The five keys to a successful Google team. https://rework.withgoogle.com/blog/five-keys-to-a-successful-google-team/, published 17 November 2015, accessed 11 August 2022.

[7] Edmondson, A. (2019). *The Fearless Organization: Creating Psychological Safety in the Workplace for Learning, Innovation, and Growth*. Hoboken, NJ: Wiley.

[8] Ibid.

[9] Ibid.

[10] Locke, E. A., & Latham, G. P. (2006). New directions in goal-setting theory. *Current Directions of Psychological Science, 15*(5), 265–268.

[11] This exercise is adapted from Sternad, D. (2020). *Effective Management: Developing Yourself, Others and Organizations*. London: Red Globe Press, p. 83.

[12] This definition of coaching is adapted from Sternad, D. (2021). *Developing Coaching Skills: A Concise Introduction*. Moosburg: econcise, p. 6.

[13] This whole section is based on Sternad, D. (2021). *Developing Coaching Skills: A Concise Introduction*. Moosburg: econcise, pp. 10–11.

[14] The following questions are based on Sternad, D. (2021). *Developing Coaching Skills: A Concise Introduction*. Moosburg: econcise, p. 28; the GROW model was popularized by Sir John Whitmore [Whitmore, Sir J. (2017). *Coaching for Performance: The Principles and Practice of Coaching and Leadership*. 5th ed. London/Boston: Nicholas Brealey Publishing.]

[15] The questions are taken and partly adapted from Sternad, D. (2021). *Developing Coaching Skills: A Concise Introduction*. Moosburg: econcise, pp. 31–36; 38–39.

[16] Sudakow, J. (2017). 6 creative ways to develop your people that don't cost any money. https://www.inc.com/james-sudakow/6-creative-ways-to-develop-your-people-that-dont-cost-any-money.html, published 10 May 2017, accessed 8 August 2022.

[17] Bailey, C., Madden, A., Alfes, K., & Fletcher, L. (2017). The meaning, antecedents and outcomes of employee engagement: A narrative synthesis. *International Journal of Management Reviews, 19*(1), 31–53.

[18] Radcliffe, S. (2012). *Leadership: Plain and Simple*. 2nd ed. Harlow: Pearson.

[19] Ibid.

[20] Sternad, D. (2020). *Effective Management: Developing Yourself, Others and Organizations*. London: Red Globe Press.

[21] Hirst, C. (2019). *No Bullsh*t Leadership*. London: Profile Books, p. 15.

[22] Sternad, D. (2020). *Effective Management: Developing Yourself, Others and Organizations*. London: Red Globe Press, p. 280.

[23] Kotter, J. P. (2007). Leading change: Why transformation efforts fail. *Harvard Business Review, 86*(7/8), 130–139; Marquet, D. L. (2020). *Leadership is Language: The Hidden Power of What You Say—and What You Don't*. London: Penguin Random House; Maxwell, J. C. (2018). *Developing the Leader Within You 2.0*. New York, NY: HarperCollins Leadership.

[24] Maxwell, J. C. (2018). *Developing the Leader Within You 2.0*. New York, NY: HarperCollins Leadership.

[25] ACECQA (2020). Meetings and reflective sessions. https://www.acecqa.gov.au/sites/default/files/2021-03/RegularMeetingsAndReflectiveSessions.pdf, accessed 11 August 2022.

[26] miro.com (n.d.). Start, stop, continue retrospective template. https://miro.com/templates/start-stop-continue-retrospective/, accessed 11 August 2022.

[27] Geys, B., Connolly, S., Kassim, H., & Murdoch, Z. (2020). Follow the leader? Leader succession and staff attitudes in public sector organizations. *Public Administration Review, 80*(4), 555–564.

[28] Maxwell, J. C. (2018). *Developing the Leader Within You 2.0*. New York, NY: HarperCollins Leadership, p. 213.

Further reading

Chapter 1 Develop a leadership mindset

01 Develop leadership presence

Fox Cabane, O. (2012). *The Charisma Myth: Master the Art of Personal Magnetism*. London: Portfolio Penguin.

Lubar, K., & Halpern, B. L. (2004). *Leadership Presence: Dramatic Techniques to Reach Out, Motivate, and Inspire*. New York, NY: Avery.

02 Show confidence

Fox Cabane, O. (2012). *The Charisma Myth: Master the Art of Personal Magnetism*. London: Portfolio Penguin.

Strycharczyk, D., Clough, P., & Perry, J. (2021). *Developing Mental Toughness: Strategies to Improve Performance, Resilience and Wellbeing in Individuals and Organizations*. 3rd ed. London: Kogan Page.

03 Spread positive energy

Gordon, J. (2017). *The Power of Positive Leadership: How and Why Positive Leaders Transform Teams and Organizations and Change the World*. Hoboken, NJ: Wiley.

04 Show that you care

Younger, H. R. (2021). *The Art of Caring Leadership: How Leading With Heart Uplifts Teams and Organizations*. San Francisco, CA: Berrett-Koehler Publishers.

05 Cultivate a growth mindset

Dweck, C. (2006). *Mindset: The New Psychology of Success*. New York, NY: Ballantine Books.

06 Control your emotions

Peters, S. (2012). *The Chimp Paradox: The Mind Management Programme for Confidence, Success and Happiness*. London: Vermilion.

07 Know your values

Kraemer Jr., H. M. J. (2011). *From Values to Action: The Four Principles of Values-Based Leadership*. San Francisco, CA: Jossey-Bass.

08 Be fully committed

Clear, J. (2018). *Atomic Habits: An Easy and Proven Way to Build Good Habits and Break Bad Ones*. London: Random House Business Books.

09 Be resilient

Maxwell, J. C. (2013). *Sometimes You Win, Sometimes You Learn: Life's Greatest Lessons Are Gained From Our Losses*. New York, NY: Center Street.

10 Make self-reflection a habit

Bailey, J. R., & Rehman, S. (2022). Don't underestimate the power of self-reflection. https://hbr.org/2022/03/dont-underestimate-the-power-of-self-reflection, published 4 March 2022, accessed 11 July 2022.

Chapter 2 Communicate with impact

11 Respect self-esteem needs

Marquet, D. L. (2020). *Leadership is Language: The Hidden Power of What You Say—and What You Don't*. London: Penguin Random House.

Watzlawick, P., Bavelas, J. B., & Jackson, D. D. (1967). *Pragmatics of Human Communication: A Study of Interactional Patterns, Pathologies and Paradoxes*. New York, NY: W. W. Norton.

12 Clarify your communication objective

Kuhnke, E. (2013). *Communication Skills for Dummies*. Chichester: John Wiley & Sons, Chapter 2: Knowing what you want to achieve.

13 Lead with questions

Marquardt, M. J. (2014). *Leading With Questions: How Leaders Find the Right Solutions by Knowing What to Ask*. San Francisco, CA: Jossey-Bass.

Robbins, A. (2001). *Awaken the Giant Within: Take Immediate Control of Your Mental, Emotional, Physical and Financial Destiny*. London: Simon & Schuster/Pocket Books, Chapter 8: Questions are the answer.

14 Practice active listening

Rogers, C. R., & Farson, R. E. (1957). *Active Listening*. Chicago, IL: Industrial Relations Center, University of Chicago.

15 Decode nonverbal signals

Navarro, J., & Sciarra Pointer, T. (2021). *Be Exceptional: Master the Five Traits that Set Extraordinary People Apart*. London: Thorsons, Chapter 2: Observation—Seeing what matters.

16 Present your ideas in a persuasive way

Barker, A. (2019). *Improve Your Communication Skills: How to Build Trust, Be Heard and Communicate With Confidence*. 5th ed. London: Kogan Page, Chapter 5: The skills of persuasion.

17 Speak to the heart

Brown, B. (2018). *Dare to Lead: Brave Work, Tough Conversations, Whole Hearts*. London: Vermilion.

18 Harness the power of feedback

Folkman, J. R. (2006). *The Power of Feedback: 35 Principles for Turning Feedback from Others Into Personal and Professional Change*. Hoboken, NY: John Wiley & Sons.

19 Master tough conversations

Patterson, K., Grenny, J., McMillan, R., & Switzler, A. (2012). *Crucial Conversations: Tools for Talking When the Stakes Are High*. 2nd ed. New York, NY: McGraw-Hill.

20 Become a master negotiator

Fisher, R., Ury, W. L., & Patton, B. (1991). *Getting to Yes: Negotiating Agreement Without Giving In*. Boston/New York: Houghton Mifflin Company.

Chapter 3 Clarify purpose and priorities

21 Have a clear purpose

Sinek, S. (2017). *Find Your Why: A Practical Guide for Discovering Purpose for You and Your Team*. New York, NY: Portfolio / Penguin.

22 Think strategically

Lafley, A. G., & Martin, R. L. (2013). *Playing to Win: How Strategy Really Works*. Boston, MA: Harvard Business Review Press.

Sola, D., & Couturier, J. (2014). *How to Think Strategically: Your Roadmap to Innovation and Results*. Harlow: Pearson Education Limited.

23 Be clear on your goals

Minto, B. (2008). *The Pyramid Principle*. 3rd ed. Harlow: Financial Times Prentice Hall.

24 Set the right priorities

McKeon, G. (2020). *Essentialism: The Disciplined Pursuit of Less*. Trade paperback edition. New York, NY: Currency.

25 Delegate with impact

Landry, L. (2020). How to delegate effectively: 9 tips for managers. https://online.hbs.edu/blog/post/how-to-delegate-effectively, published 14 January 2020, accessed 23 December 2022.

Sternad, D. (2020). *Effective Management: Developing Yourself, Others and Organizations*. London: Red Globe Press.

26 Solve problems

Sternad, D. (2021). *Solve It! The Mindset and Tools of Smart Problem Solvers*. Moosburg: econcise.

27 Make better decisions

Hammond, J. S., Keeney, R. L., & Raiffa, H. (2015). *Smart Choices: A Practical Guide to Making Better Decisions*. Boston, MA: Harvard Business Review Press.

28 Identify the bottleneck

Goldratt, E. M., & Goldratt-Ashlag, E. (2010). *The Choice*. Revised ed. Great Barrington, MA: North River Press.

29 Eliminate the nonessentials

Hyatt, M. (2019). *Free to Focus: A Total Productivity System to Achieve More By Doing Less*. Grand Rapids, MI: Baker Books.

30 Use your time wisely

Burkeman, O. (2021). *Four Thousand Weeks: Time and How to Use It*. London: The Bodley Head.

Chapter 4 Build a winning team

31 Get the right people into your team

Bryant, A. (n.d.). How to hire the right person. https://www.nytimes.com/guides/business/how-to-hire-the-right-person, accessed 8 October 2022.

32 Clarify roles and rules

Belbin, R. M. (2012). *Team Roles at Work*. 2nd ed. London: Routledge.

33 Establish trust and rapport

Citrin, J. M., & DeRosa, D. (2021). No trust, no team: Six best practices for building trust on virtual teams. https://www.spencerstuart.com/leadership-matters/2021/march/no-trust-no-team, published 25 March 2021, accessed 19 August 2022.

Timms, M. (2022). 5 ways leaders can build trust no matter where their teams work. https://www.fastcompany.com/90728111/5-ways-leaders-can-build-trust-no-matter-where-their-teams-work, published 10 March 2022, accessed 19 August 2022.

34 Ensure accountability

Patterson, K., Grenny, J., Maxfield, D., McMillan, R., & Switzler, A. (2013). *Crucial Accountability: Tools for Resolving Violated Expectations, Broken Commitments, and Bad Behavior*. 2nd ed. New York, NY: McGraw Hill.

35 Make meetings productive

Sternad, D. (2020). *Effective Management: Developing Yourself, Others and Organizations*. London: Red Globe Press.

36 Lead a virtual team

Citrin, J. M., & DeRosa, D. (2021). *Leading at a Distance: Practical Lessons for Virtual Success*. Hoboken, NY: John Wiley & Sons.

Hanabury, E., & Stoddart, L. (2020). How to lead virtual teams successfully. https://www8.gsb.columbia.edu/articles/columbia-business/how-lead-virtual-teams-successfully, published 28 May 2020, accessed 17 August 2022.

Powers, H. (2018). *Virtual Teams for Dummies*. Hoboken, NY: John Wiley & Sons.

37 Create an agile team

Clayton, S. J. (2021). An agile approach to change management. *Harvard Business Review*. https://hbr.org/2021/01/an-agile-approach-to-change-management, published 12 January 2021, accessed 1 July 2022.

scrum.org (n.d.). What is scrum? https://www.scrum.org/resources/what-is-scrum, accessed 17 August 2022.

38 Manage conflicts

Kotter, J. P. (2007). Leading change: Why transformation efforts fail. *Harvard Business Review, 86*(7/8), 130–139.

Maxwell. J. C. (2018). *Developing the Leader Within You 2.0*. New York, NY: HarperCollins Leadership.

39 Create and maintain a team spirit

Heermann, B. (1997). *Building Team Spirit: Activities for Inspiring and Energizing Teams*. New York, NY: McGraw-Hill.

40 Cultivate your extended team

Zack, D. (2019). *Networking for People Who Hate Networking: A Field Guide for Introverts, the Overwhelmed, and the Underconnected*. 2nd ed. Oakland, CA: Berrett-Koehler Publishers.

Chapter 5 Help others grow

41 Recognize their strengths

Rath, T., & Conchie, B. (2009). *Strengths Based Leadership: Great Leaders, Teams, and Why People Follow*. New York, NY: Gallup Press.

42 Create a fear-free environment

Edmondson, A. (2019). *The Fearless Organization: Creating Psychological Safety in the Workplace for Learning, Innovation, and Growth*. Hoboken, NJ: Wiley.

43 Provide challenges

Locke, E. A., & Latham, G. P. (2006). New directions in goal-setting theory. *Current Directions of Psychological Science, 15*(5), 265-268.

Sternad, D. (2020). *Effective Management: Developing Yourself, Others and Organizations*. London: Red Globe Press.

44 Coach your team members

Sternad, D. (2021). *Developing Coaching Skills: A Concise Introduction*. Moosburg: econcise.

Whitmore, Sir J. (2017). *Coaching for Performance: The Principles and Practice of Coaching and Leadership*. 5th ed. London/Boston: Nicholas Brealey Publishing.

45 Create learning and development opportunities

Sudakow, J. (2017). 6 creative ways to develop your people that don't cost any money. https://www.inc.com/james-sudakow/6-creative-ways-to-develop-your-people-that-dont-cost-any-money.html, published 10 May 2017, accessed 8 August 2022.

Swanson, R. A. (2022). *Foundations of Human Resource Development.* 3rd ed. Oakland, CA: Berrett-Koehler.

46 Engage your team members

Radcliffe, S. (2012). *Leadership: Plain and Simple.* 2nd ed. Harlow: Pearson.

47 Address performance problems

Sternad, D. (2020). *Effective Management: Developing Yourself, Others and Organizations.* London: Red Globe Press.

48 Manage change

Kotter, J. P. (2007). Leading change: Why transformation efforts fail. *Harvard Business Review, 86*(7/8), 130–139.

Maxwell. J. C. (2018). *Developing the Leader Within You 2.0.* New York, NY: HarperCollins Leadership.

49 Organize reflective sessions

Derby, E., & Larsen, D. (2006). *Agile Retrospectives: Making Good Teams Great.* Dallas, TX/Raleigh, NC: The Pragmatic Bookshelf.

50 Be a role model in developing yourself

Belton, S. (2021). *Change Your Life in 5: Practical Steps to Making Meaningful Changes in Your Life.* London: Orange Hippo!

Index

About the author and illustrator

Dr Dietmar Sternad is an award-winning management professor and bestselling author with extensive experience in various leadership roles (e.g. as a CEO of media companies) as well as in educating and coaching new and experienced leaders. He has published numerous research articles, case studies, and textbooks (including the international bestsellers *Developing Coaching Skills* and *Solve It! The Mindset and Tools of Smart Problem Solvers*, both published by econcise).

Eva Kobin is a self-taught artist passionate about graphical facilitation and illustration. The pursuit of her dream made her leave her little village in Estonia and continue management studies in Austria, where she met Dietmar. Art helped her with her master's degree, bringing simplicity and a little humor, even for the topics that initially seemed difficult. With her little characters, she brings a funny side to otherwise serious management topics. Hopefully, you will enjoy her drawings as much as she did creating them for you!

Apply the strategies and tools of smart problem solving—and succeed in work and life!

What do Albert Einstein, Elon Musk, Sherlock Holmes, and Mahatma Gandhi's six-year old granddaughter have in common?
They are all masters of **the art of smart problem solving—** a highly sought-after skill that you can learn too!

Solve It! The Mindset and Tools of Smart Problem Solvers
by Dietmar Sternad
is available wherever good books and ebooks are sold.